S0-BKK-247

THE HOCKEY EXPLOSION

BY BILL GUTMAN

tempo
books

GROSSET & DUNLAP, INC.
A National General Company
Publishers   New York

DEDICATION

For Elizabeth, the painter and gardener who saved me hours of time.

■

ACKNOWLEDGMENTS

The author would like to thank the National Hockey League and many of its member teams for providing background material for this book. Thanks also to the many writers who have recorded the great moments in the ice game for all to read and enjoy. And a nod to the hearty breed of hockey players who have brought their skills and unique personalities to the world's fastest growing sport.

A special thanks to Al Greenberg for providing insight into the hockey explosion from a true fan's point of view, and for taking the time to relate many of his personal experiences as a guy who really lives the game.

Contents

Introduction

THE PROFESSIONAL HOCKEY player is a rugged individualist, an uncomplaining athlete who plays his sport under the most adverse conditions. He's loyal and determined, a battler who'll fight when provoked, and go to any lengths to play and win. He's a man born to demanding traditions and raised to carry them out.

Not surprisingly, the true hockey fan is also a special breed. And like the players he follows, the fan is tough and determined, with a loyalty sometimes bordering on fanaticism. No, he's not insulted by that description. Tell him he's a fanatic and he'll smile proudly.

Take the case of Al Greenberg, a New York City-based businessman now in his early thirties. Greenberg isn't old enough to have seen the early epic heroes of the ice, but he knows every detail about them and their deeds.

Al's career as a hockey fan began back in 1957, when he was a high-schooler. "I went to the Rangers' first home game of the season that year," he recalls. "I enjoyed myself so much that I was back two nights later for game two. I was already hooked. From that point on I went to every home game and I've rarely missed one since. You might say my career began at the same time Bobby Hull's did. He was a rookie with the Black Hawks that year, and played his first game against the Rangers at the Garden."

It wasn't long before Greenberg discovered the handicaps of following a sport that still hadn't found national or popular acceptance. "There was no radio or television coverage then, so following the away games was a problem. It became a challenge to try to pick up stations late at night on a transistor radio. I used to listen to Boston without any problem, and when I was lucky, Chicago. Montreal came in, too, but the announcer spoke in French. I didn't understand a word of it, but still managed to follow the action by listening for the players' names. And when there was a score, the P.A. announcer broadcast in both French and English."

But sitting by a radio didn't satisfy Al Greenberg. He needed action. Before long, he started making the trek to the other NHL cities. "I wasn't old enough to drive a car, but I could hitchhike. Detroit and Chicago were a bit too far, but Boston was easy to get to, and I also made it up to both Toronto and Montreal."

That still wasn't enough hockey for Al Greenberg. He took to seeking out minor league games when the pros didn't play, and his thumb began taking him to places like Hershey, Pa.; Providence, R.I.; Springfield, Mass.; and Baltimore, Md.—American Hockey League cities, Al also went to see even humbler Eastern League games all along the east coast.

He often planned his trips so he could take in an NHL game in Boston one night, and an American League game in Springfield or Providence the next afternoon. And the more games he saw, the more trips he started to make. Some days he returned to school with the bleary-eyed look of one who has had no sleep. Slowly, but surely, his whole lifestyle began revolving around hockey; his Bible was the master schedule of the NHL and minor league teams.

"It was during my college days (in New York City) that I completed one of the greatest parlays of my life," he says, with fond remembrance. "I took in a Ranger game at Madison Square Garden on Sunday night. Monday I was in Hershey for an AHL game. Tuesday I went over to Jersey to watch the Jersey Larks of the Eastern League. Wednesday I was back in the Garden and Thursday it was up to Boston. The whole thing happened during Christmas of 1960 and it made a great present, if I say so myself."

His hockey fever grew worse, and pretty soon Al Greenberg found the game controlling his entire destiny. But he didn't mind.

"You may not believe this, but I actually scheduled my wedding for mid-January, when the Rangers were on a long road trip. My honeymoon ended the day they got back to town."

Like most hockey players, hockey fan Al Greenberg has set goals for himself. His two major goals evolved slowly during the mid-1960's.

"My first goal is to see the Rangers win the Stanley Cup," he confesses. "I've got a theory about this and it may sound depressing. The Rangers last won the cup in 1940, the year before I was born. And the more I see the more I'm convinced the next time they'll win it will be the year after I die. But I'll keep trying.

"The second goal—and this one has been made a lot harder since expansion—is to see a National Hockey League game in every city where there's a team. The original six cities were easy. So were some of the others. As of now, the only places I haven't been are St. Louis and Vancouver. But I'll get there somehow, believe me."

You may ask how Greenberg could get to places like Los Angeles and Oakland, let alone Chicago, Detroit, Toronto, etc., while working at a steady job.

"Fortunately," he says, "the job I used to have involved a lot of traveling. I was pretty much on my own as to when I could go, and I always set up my business trips around The Schedule so I could take in a game at the same time. It was a great arrangement, although stometimes I had a tough time explaining why I *had* to come on a certain day.

"Other times, the logistics weren't easy. I had one trip to Buffalo (before the NHL Sabres were in town) and wanted to get up to Toronto to see the Rangers play a crucial game there. I rented a car and drove from Buffalo to Toronto in a bad snowstorm. It was no fun, but the Rangers won, 2-1, so the trip was well worth it."

Greenberg's fanatic trip to Toronto parallels one made by old-time Bruin defenseman Eddie Shore, who once missed a train and drove from Boston to Montreal in a blizzard just so he could play in the game.

As a hockey nut of almost two decades standing, Al Greenberg has witnessed the hockey explosion first hand.

"Seats were cheap when I first started going," he says. "Something like fifty cents for the side balcony in the old Garden. There was an unwritten law then that if you got there early and slapped the seats down (the ushers put them all up before a game) no one would take them. You could then go out for a bite of supper before returning and your seats would still be there.

"Sometimes a group of guys would get there early, slap their seats down, then go out in the corridors and play their own game of hockey with a paper cup as a puck and their feet as sticks. The games were unbelievably rough. Guys would kick and check each other and you'd raise a real sweat. I remember one game when we went out to play between periods. A friend of mine got hit hard and broke his nose. He was bleeding all over the place, but he refused medical aid and returned to his seat to watch the rest of the game. I guess the ice traditions extended right to the fans in those days.

"As the years went on, prices rose and the old non-reserved seats, the ones we slapped down, became reserved only. Students and youngsters were shut out by inflation and more stolid types began occupying the same areas. But in the old days, the fans brawled as often as the players.

"It was a real scramble when playoff tickets went on sale," Al said. "We used to line up at 11 P.M. and stand there all night, sometimes in the rain or snow. Fights would break out all the time as people jockeyed for position, with maybe 5,000 or more fans trying to get 2,000 seats. It became so bad that I finally said the heck with it and bought season tickets."

Al Greenberg wasn't the only rabid fan of the ice game. He had many friends who did the same thing, and he would see some of the same people hanging around year after year.

"I remember when I was still in college, seeing this guy at all the games. In fact, I saw him everywhere. Whenever we'd go up to a practice session he'd be there, and whenever we'd make a road trip with the Ranger fan club he was along. It was like he spent his entire day as close to the action and the players as he could. I was a student and had spare time, but I always wondered what this guy did, whether he worked or not, and what kind of a job he had that gave him all the free time.

"Then I found out. He was a Good Humor man, sold ice cream, because he'd only have to work in the summer months. That freed him for the entire hockey season and I knew then what lengths people would go to if they loved the sport."

Al Greenberg still attends the games. He loves the Rangers as much as ever, but he has noticed the effects of the hockey explosion on the game and its fans.

"First of all, you don't see as many exciting games as you did when it was a six-team league. Then, there was very little difference between the best and the worst. You always saw exciting play. Today, many games are one-sided as the talent is spread thin and there are more very weak teams.

"As for the players, I think the biggest change has been in goaltending. With six teams it was a hard fraternity to crack. There were six goalies; they played every game and were usually veterans over 30 years old. Now each team has two, sometimes three goalies. They all wear masks so you don't see their faces and can't identify with them as closely. And many of them certainly aren't as proficient as those original, courageous six men.

"There's one big difference I notice at games. All the noise comes from the balcony. The downstairs seats are occupied by a lot of businessmen who don't really care about the game as pure sport. They may be entertaining clients, or they're there because it's fashionable. And when there's an unimportant game or a bad team in, many of the lower boxes will be empty, while the upstairs is still jammed with the old-time fans. They haven't changed at all."

Much of Al Greenberg's life still revolves around hockey. He's promised his wife that he'll stop going when the Rangers win the Cup. But, because of his depressing hunch about when that will happen, Al feels pretty safe in making the promise.

In the meantime, the game he loves keeps growing. Many things have changed in hockey, but many remain the same. This book delves into the game, its origins, its traditions, and its players, and it may help you understand why the world's fastest sport has such a strange hold on so many people. Just one word of caution . . . Beware, it could happen to you.

1   *How It All Began*

ICE HOCKEY IS a Canadian game. It started north of the border and has been the national sport in that country ever since. Yet in the past decade, the flashing skates of the National Hockey League stars have streaked across the United States from coast to coast. Now, with one added competition of the new World Hockey Association, we truly have a hockey explosion.

Not only has there been a proliferation of big league teams, but the sport has grown on other levels as well. Pee Wee Leagues are springing up everywhere. More hockey camps are opening their doors every year. High schools have joined in the competition and American colleges are breeding their own players who are slowly filtering into the pros, a feat at one time reserved only for Canadian-born athletes.

In fact, developments in recent years have brought some grumblings from the north. Canadian purists are saying the United States is ruining their game. Most of the new franchises are in the U.S., not in Canada, though Montreal, Quebec, Toronto, Winnipeg, and

Vancouver are all represented. But America is where the money is, where the sports-crazy public has the time and means to attend games, and where television can provide revenues unheard of just ten or 15 years ago.

Up to that time, hockey players were grossly underpaid, especially when compared with athletes in baseball, football, and basketball. Now, they've more than made up the difference. With the established National Hockey League bidding to keep its talent away from the fledgling World Hockey Association, the price has gone up. Many players who would have had a hard time making the old six-team NHL are now commanding six-figure salaries lest they be pirated away to the other league.

In addition, endorsements and personal appearances are on the rise. Rocket Richard and Gordie Howe were two of hockey's biggest stars in the 40's and 50's, yet they earned less than $20,000 annually for most of their careers, and were known only to avid NHL fans. Today, players like Bobby Orr, Bobby Hull, Derek Anderson, Phil Esposito, Bobby Clarke, Brad Park, and Ed Giacomin are almost as familiar to most Americans as Dick Allen, John Unitas, and Jerry West.

How did it all happen? What made this game of Canada move south of the border? And what was it like way back when? Let's go back to the beginnings, before people knew about right wingers, goalies, faceoffs, high-sticking, and the rest of the terms indigenous to what has often been called the world's fastest sport.

The modern game of ice hockey slowly evolved in Canada during the middle and late nineteenth century. So disjointed and vague are those beginnings, that even the old timers don't know where the very first hockey game was played.

Some people around Kingston in the province of Ontario, and Halifax in Nova Scotia, argue that the sport originated and was first played in their cities. But there is little documentary evidence to back up such claims.

Another version has it that students at McGill University in Montreal organized the first crude game in early 1875. It is certain that the sport did grow very quickly in and around the French-speaking city, and the partisans of Montreal have always considered the game more or less their own.

One thing is for sure. Hockey in those days was a very different sport from the one we know today. First of all, the game was played outdoors. There were no arenas with artificial ice. Rinks were either hacked out between snowbanks or were those originally created for leisurely pleasure skating. There were no boards surrounding the rinks and the changing weather patterns sometimes left the ice in abominable condition. One rink used for hockey even had a complete bandstand occupying center ice, and the players had to go around it.

Sticks were nothing more than rough pieces of wood. The puck, too, was made of wood. Early teams had nine men on the ice at once, and even when the number dropped to seven, those seven usually played the entire contest, which consisted of two 30-minute halves. There were a couple of subs, but they only got in if there was a serious injury.

The referee had no uniform, just his own hat and coat, and he carried a large bell rather than a whistle. Goalies not only didn't wear masks, but they scorned the use of any pads or protection. The goal was simply a set of four-foot stakes, placed six feet apart. The crossbar and net had not yet come into existence. The goal judge sat behind the goal and waved a handkerchief to indicate a score.

Goalies had to play standing up. No flopping around or even dropping to the knees was allowed. Naturally, they couldn't dive after a flying puck and that eliminated the possibility of the spectacular saves that occur so often today. In that respect, it was harder to defend the goal. At the same time, however, it was harder for the offense to score. Forward passes were against the rules and so were shots off a rebound. The two defensemen had to line up one behind the other and couldn't leave their zones.

Forwards, too, had to play their positions or lanes, and they were the only ones allowed to carry the puck. A fourth forward, called a rover, had a big advantage over everyone else. He could go anywhere, and teams usually put their best skater and player in this position.

At first, none of the players were paid. Any profit from admission fees or contributions went to the rink owners. But the game spread across Canada just the same, and many more Canadian boys began putting on the skates, making their own sticks and pucks, and playing this new, exciting ice game.

It didn't take long before public interest was generated in the new sport. Some of the most distinguished men of Canada became fans of the local teams that had, by then, been organized in their communities.

In 1890, one such Canadian, Arthur Stanley, was instrumental in founding the Ontario Hockey Association. It was a loosely organized group of teams that began playing each other on a regular basis. Some clubs, such as Ottawa City, had powerful teams even then, garnering all the local talent from the area. Other clubs were put together from less typical backgrounds.

One such team was the Rideau Rebels, named for Rideau Hall in Ottawa. Rideau Hall was the Government House where the Governor General of Canada resided. In 1888, Lord Frederick Arthur Stanley became Governor General. Arthur Stanley was his son. And when the Stanley boys, Arthur and Algie, became avid hockey buffs, they formed the Rebels, consisting of sons and friends of the Government officials. They were a surprisingly tough bunch, and held their own against the people's clubs such as Ottawa City.

By the time Arthur Stanley formed the Ontario Hockey Association, his father had also become a rabid follower of the ice game. In fact, when Lord Stanley and his sons returned to England for a visit, they arranged a game of ice hockey at Buckingham Palace. Playing against the Stanley boys that day were the Prince of Wales (later King Edward VII) and the Duke of York (later King George V). So the game was known to royalty at the same time that it spread among the masses.

But organizing that famous encounter wasn't all Lord Stanley did for the ice game. He wanted to make some permanent contribution in Canada, even though he himself had returned to England to turn his duties over to a successor. So he drafted a letter to his aide, Lord Kilcoursie, which read in part as follows:

"I have for some time been thinking it would be a good thing if there were a challenge cup which could be held from year to year by the leading hockey club in Canada. There does not appear to be any outward or visible sign of the championship at present. Considering the interest that hockey matches now elicit and the importance of having the games fairly played under generally organized rules, I am willing to give a cup that shall be annually held by the winning club."

Lord Stanley didn't waste any time implementing his idea. He had a silver cup struck for 10 guineas, roughly $50—a lot of money in those days—and offered it to the team proving itself the best in hockey during the 1894 season. The Stanley Cup, as the trophy quickly came to be known, served as a unifying force that eventually resulted in the formation of the National Hockey League.

Today the cup goes to the winner of the post-season playoffs in the National Hockey League and is emblematic of the world's championship. (The new World Hockey Association has its own trophy, the World Cup.)

In the early years of the twentieth century, the various teams and leagues in Canada began showing more organization and desire for organization. Fans wanted to see natural rivalries continue in addition to seeing their favorite stars perform regularly. Obviously, games arranged and scheduled in advance made for a better sport.

In 1899, a man named Arthur Farrell of the Shamrock Hockey Club drew up the first set of formalized hockey rules and this, too, had helped stabilize the game. Farrell's rules called for seven men on a team and a rink at least 112 feet long and 58 feet wide (as compared to today's minimum of 200 feet by 85 feet.

For a decade and a half the teams in various leagues throughout Canada continued to play with the one unifying goal—the Stanley Cup. All teams worked toward the chance to challenge last year's winner. And although the Cup was hockey's top prize, other changes taking place within the game were moving it forward, too.

By the turn of the century, the game was booming in Canada and every community, no matter how small or remote, had its local teams. Sooner or later those teams attempted to enter leagues. When they couldn't get into existing leagues, they formed new ones.

Local rivalries became intense, and before long there was more than a casual effort to attract the best players. If the local community couldn't produce them, then they'd have to come from somewhere else. It was the beginning of the professional hockey player, but it came in a roundabout way. Players were given high-paying jobs in the community which they worked at part of the time. The real reason they were there was to play hockey, however, and they were given plenty of time to practice for the games. Soon after that, as the competition for players increased, additional sums of money began to exchange hands, much of it under the table because the leagues were still considered amateur.

Soon a regular pattern emerged. Teams which played in the larger arenas and in the big cities were demanding a share of the receipts from rink owners, and they were getting it. In 1902, a Federal Hockey League was organized in the United States. The league didn't last, but when it started the organizers began looking north for players. It didn't take much to get Canadian players to give up their amateur status for cold cash. It was obvious that something had to be done. The Canadian owners anted up.

New Canadian leagues continued to come and go in the early days of the century, and more often than not, an entire league would be dissolved just to get rid of one team or a tempestuous owner. Then, around 1906, a new league was formed, the National Hockey Association, with seven teams, three of them playing out of Montreal. This league was a direct forebear of the NHL.

The league not only played in Montreal, but also in the outlying silver mining camps that had sprung up around 1905. Huge crowds jammed into small rinks and bets were made as fast as the people could talk.

More rule changes were occurring. In 1909 the game was changed from two 30-minute halves to three 20-minute periods. At about the same time, NHA teams adopted six-man hockey, eliminating the old rover man. Yet on the west coast of Canada, in the newly formed Pacific League, seven-man hockey remained.

Just prior to World War I, more rule changes occurred that brought the game much closer to what it is today. Free substitution during play was allowed for the first time, a goal line was put on the ice, refs began dropping the puck for face-offs, and there were new definitions of major and minor penalties in an attempt to eliminate some of the unwarranted roughing-up of opposing players.

The War slowed the progress the NHA had made. Many players left to enlist, and team rosters were a shambles. In fact, there were so many players in uniform that, in 1917, the 228th Battalion entered a team in the NHA and whipped through the first half of the schedule.

In late 1916, NHA owners held another meeting and it was suddenly announced that the league had been dissolved. The new National Hockey League was created in it place. The move was for a reason quite usual in early hockey. The owners wanted to get rid of the owner of the Toronto Blueshirts, a man named Eddie Livingston, and by forming a new league that didn't include his team, they found a way to do it. Frank Calder was the first president of the new league and a new Toronto team, the Arenas, replaced Livingston's Blueshirts.

There were five teams in the NHL that first year, the Montreal Canadiens, Montreal Wanderers, Ottawa, Quebec, and Toronto. Only Toronto had artificial ice. Yet fans didn't take to the new NHL. In fact, western hockey, which kept the old seven-man game, was edging ahead of eastern hockey in popularity. There were other troubles, too. Without warning, the Quebec team disbanded. Then a fire destroyed the Montreal Wanderers' arena, finishing that club. When the season ended, just three teams remained in the league.

Joe Malone of the Canadiens won the scoring title that year by netting 44 goals in just 20 games, a percentage record that's never been equaled.

In the Stanley Cup playoffs that year it became obvious that all of hockey had to standarize its rules. Goalies were now allowed to sprawl and dive, and the new rule immediately made Ottawa's Clint Benedict the best net-minder in the league. Teams also had to play shorthanded during penalties, and new rules regarding the forward pass were adopted. Although there were endless hassles over the different sets of rules when the western teams came to play for the Cup, through it all, hockey was slowly finding its way into a new, modern age.

The 1918–19 season had just an 18-game schedule, and the playoffs had to be suspended when a flu epidemic spread, striking down the exhausted players like flies.

For the next several years the league worked hard to get on solid ground. Teams dropped out and new ones entered. Schedules were altered and expanded, as the National Hockey League began finding its way. Here are some of the highlights.

In 1919–20, the clubs played a 24-game schedule, the most extensive ever. It was increased to 30 games in 1924–25, a year that marked the first American entry in the league—the Boston Bruins.

A year later two more American teams entered the league, the New York Americans and the Pittsburgh Pirates. And the year after that came the New York Rangers, Chicago Black Hawks, and Detroit Cougars. There were now two five-team divisions in the NHL and the schedule was upped to 44 games. And for the first time, the Stanley Cup became the exclusive property of the National Hockey League, which was now considered *the* major league of all hockey.

So things were pretty much set. There were still some franchise shifts up to 1942, when the permanent six-team alignment was formed. The NHL remained in that form until the big expansion of 1967. Hockey had come a long way since those early days in the nineteenth century. Now it's time to take a look at the men who helped the game grow in those early years.

2 Hockey Players—Old Style

WHAT MAKES A hockey player? It's no secret that he's a unique kind of athlete. He's born and bred in a certain way, geared to life on ice and to a brutal and bruising sport. Uncomplaining, he often takes to the ice with every ailment imaginable and, more often than not, plays as if he isn't even hurt. Hockey players continue to perform with injuries that would sideline their counterparts in baseball, football and basketball.

In the 1970's this may change. There are indications that hockey players starting out in the 1970's may be different from the players of the present and the past.

Some things never change. The traditional hockey player has been on ice skates almost as long as he's been walking. By the time he was perhaps ten years old, he began collecting the standard injuries, such as missing or broken teeth. And he had learned that it was part of the game.

The typical hockey player is still a Canadian, and hockey is to Canada as baseball is to the United States.

Canadian youngsters play hockey not only in the big cities, but in the smallest of towns. Just look at the rosters of big league hockey teams and you'll get an idea about how far in the bush some of them come from: South Porcupine, Ontario; Trail, British Columbia; and Central Butte, Saskatchewan.

In Canada, youngsters playing in the Pee Wee, Bantam, and Little Leagues play strict National Hockey League rules with full checking allowed all over the ice. So the Canadian kid learns to play tough and win. Young players learn to take it well as well as dish it out, and their coaches drum this into their heads constantly.

It's always been harder for Americans. For one thing, great areas of the United States do not have natural ice, so far fewer kids play hockey. For another, American hockey for kids is not as punishing. Many high schools in the United States have restrictions on where and when checking can take place in their games.

Another change that may influence the hockey of the future took place in 1967. Prior to an NHL ruling that year, which prohibited signing a player until he reached 20, most youngsters were under the gun from an early age. There was real pressure. The coaches at the most elementary levels were in the business of making future pros. And a pro team could put its mark on a youngster when he reached 14. At the age of 14, kids could sign letters of intent which bound them to a pro team immediately, giving that team the only shot at signing him if he developed into a pro performer. Bobby Orr and Bobby Hull were both signed this way.

Hull, in fact, was so good at age 14, that the Chicago Black Hawks (with whom he signed a letter of intent) sent him to a boarding school some 150 miles from his home where he could learn to play a better brand of hockey.

"We played something like 60 games a year," Hull recalls. "I used to get up at five in the morning to practice, and get home late at night after our games. In the beginning I cried myself to sleep at night because I missed my parents. Later, they'd come to visit me on weekends."

In effect, Bobby Hull was a professional hockey player from the time he was 14 years old. Education, like everything else, was a distant second.

The system may have been good for obtaining first-rate hockey stars, but it had some bad side effects. Suppose a boy who was grabbed at 14 didn't make it. He might keep trying until he was in his early or middle 20's. Then he'd be left with nothing, not even a high-school education. Yet many of the youngsters in those days came from such humble origins that they didn't care what might happen in 10 or 15 years. They were getting a chance to make it to the NHL and that was all that mattered.

But the players who did make it were a special breed, and this was true from the 1920's right to expansion in 1967. And even though things have changed radically since then, many of the old ways continue to survive.

For instance, the hockey player still ignores injuries that would sideline players in most other sports. How many times have you seen a player leave the ice with a bad gash or other seemingly serious injury only to return when the next period begins? Plenty. They'll lose the respect of their mates and coaches if they don't.

It's said that one NHL goaltender, who had won himself the top job, lost it again when he refused to continue after an injury. The coach turned back to his old net-minder and the injured goalie was soon traded away.

And players will often ignore injuries suffered by teammates or opponents. "Hockey players never complain," said one prominent doctor who has treated athletes in all sports. "They seem to have an extremely high threshold of pain and are determined to keep playing. It's almost a challenge to them to play through injuries. Sitting out a game is tantamount to quitting."

On the whole hockey players have always been smaller men than their counterparts in the other major sports. A 190–pound hockey man is considered a big guy, and for years, the 5' 9", 170-pounders were more or less average. Only in the last decade have bigger players become numerous in the league.

But the hockey player has always been extremely strong and well-muscled. Since most of them have spent the greater part of their lives on skates, their legs are extremely well-developed and durable. And because of the "give" the leg has on skates, they have a few serious knee and ankle injuries. So players are rarely sidelined with leg ailments such as a muscle pull or tear, unless it happens on a freak play.

Thus the common characteristics have continued down through the years. A look at the early days of the NHL will indicate the kinds of footsteps today's players must try to fill.

The National Hockey League wasn't yet firmly established at the outset of the 1920's. Amateur hockey was still very popular in Canada and was just as highly organized as the professional game. There was even an equivalent to the Stanley Cup, a trophy called the Allan Cup, which went to the best amateur team in the land.

Many highly industrialized towns had fine rinks and

could guarantee the players work and good wages off the ice. And since amateur hockey players were celebrities in Canada, the life wasn't bad at all. The same kind of popular reverence was given to junior players. In their race for the Memorial Cup, they often played to capacity crowds. Good hockey was played throughout the country, not just in the NHL towns.

In order to continue signing the best players, NHL owners had to pay large salaries, and this was one reason so many clubs folded in those early days. The Ottawa Senators were a perfect example. They had a superior team, but financial problems and the unreliability of their natural ice rink brought them to an early collapse.

Yet the level of competition in the NHL and the intensity with which the players gave of themselves was already well known by the early 1920's. When the influenza epidemic hit the Canadiens during the 1919 playoffs, the stricken Montreal players continued to give everything they had on the ice until they literally collapsed. Five were hospitalized. One—Joe Hall, a defenseman had played himself into such an exhausted state that he had no resistance to the disease and it took his life.

One of the earliest of the National Hockey League legends was Georges Vezina, a handsome Frenchman from the little town of Chicoutimi, Quebec. Vezina's name might sound familiar to hockey fans and well it should. He was a goaltender, a great one, and the Vezina Trophy, given annually to the goalie with the lowest goals-against average, is named in his honor.

Like so many Canadian youngsters, Vezina learned his hockey in his hometown, playing with the local team which had heavy support from the community. But Vezina learned in a strange way. He didn't like skates, and he played goal in his shoes. The rules were so loose in those days that it was permitted. Georges continued to play skateless until two years before he was discovered by the Montreal Canadiens. At that point someone convinced him that he should don the blades.

Vezina was discovered in February of 1910, when Les Canadiens were playing the Chicoutimi club in an exhibition game. The Montrealers figured it would be a laugher, a fun tune-up for the season ahead. After all, Chicoutimi was just an amateur team made up of part-timers and players who never would go any further.

When Vezina came out into the goal he looked calm, almost uninterested, leaning against the goalpost, his flashing eyes scanning the crowd and casually glancing at the Canadien players whom most amateurs held in awe.

Then the game started. As expected, the Canadiens dominated the action, controlling the puck, and rushing up ice with ease. It wasn't until they burst into Chicoutimi territory that the laconic goaltender came to life. But when he did, Vezina stopped everything the veteran Montreal team fired at him, displaying a cat-like quickness, and a coolness that had the pros staring in disbelief.

Midway through the second period, the Chicoutimi club had managed a pair of goals and held a 2-0 lead. The fans couldn't believe their eyes, but Vezina continued to thwart every Canadien thrust. Joe Cattarinich, the Montreal goalie and manager, urged his team on, embarrassed that the unknown youngster was chewing them up. The Montreal team got its adrenalin flowing and began playing as if it were the Stanley Cup final.

In the last period, Vezina received little support

from his exhausted teammates. It became a shooting gallery, the swift Montreal skaters trying desperately to put the puck past the young goaltender. But Vezina wouldn't yield. He parried shot after shot, and when the game ended the proud Canadiens hadn't scored a single goal!

It didn't take the Montreal management long to forget the game and go after the goalie. Georges Vezina played his first game for Les Canadiens in December 1910. He remained with the team until November 29, 1925, and in that period of 15 years, the remarkable Vezina never missed a single hockey game.

He was remarkable in other ways, too. In a rather bawdy age, Vezina was a puritan. He never smoked or drank, and certainly didn't carouse. He was also a trusting soul who never signed a formal contract with the Canadiens. A handshake from the man in charge was good enough for him.

His debut wasn't the great spectacle that his exhibition win over the Canadiens had been. He lost to Ottawa, 5-3, but by the time the 1910 season ended, the 22-year-old Vezina was leading the league with a 3.9 goals-against average as his club finished second in the league to Ottawa.

There were many goaltending highlights in Vezina's career. He was a gentle man in a brutal sport, yet he never gave any less than 100 percent and when he had to take his share of punishment he did it without complaint.

In the 1916 Stalnley Club final against the Portland Rosebuds of the Pacific Coast Association, Venzina played almost perfect goal as he turned away shot after shot, giving the Canadiens a 2-1 victory in the fifth and final game. It was just one of several Stanley Cup triumphs for which he was personally responsible.

But aside from his great goaltending, it was his charm, intelligence, and personality that made Vezina so great. Although he had little formal education, he taught himself a variety of subjects and he often gave thought to the serious aspects of life, sometimes relating them to his sport. He once wrote an essay which a teammate translated into English:

"Athletes and sportsmen rejoice in this . . . Around this outstanding British inheritance of two words—fair play—revolves Canada's powerful and precious asset, sport. It serves unfailingly, more than anything else, to impress Canadian youth with the importance of fair play. With those two words always in mind we are assured of what every thoughtful Canadian is striving for, and that is unity.

"That sport, more than anything else, can bring this about was never brought home to me more forcibly than last year on our training trip to Grimsby, Ontario. I, a French-Canadian . . . being unable to speak English and living amongst men of a different creed and racial background, made many fast friends in Ontario, friends whom I would never have known if I had not been connected with the sport of hockey."

It's not something you'd expect from a hockey player, circa 1920. And Vezina certainly saw his share of the other side of the sport. During the 1922–23 season, he was playing at Hamilton when an opposing player slammed into him, ramming him back into the post. Vezina's head was slashed open and his nose broken, yet he continued to play in the goal. Several games later, still feeling the effects of the injury, he turned back 79 Ottawa shots, allowing just one goal in a Canadien victory.

Vezina remained amazingly calm in these situations —a calm described by one writer as being "not of this world." After one typical game, a reporter wrote, "he left the rink a solemn, plodding figure, in sharp contrast to the wild hilarity of his teammates, who were already celebrating the victory that Vezina had won for them."

Although Vezina was playing first-rate hockey in 1923, he was having disturbing physical problems. He would break out in a sweat for no apparent reason, and those around him thought he was having occasional pain, although he never admitted it. Vezina continued to play his usual brand of hockey.

In the 1923–24 season, the Canadiens finished second to Ottawa, with Vezina giving up just 48 goals in 24 games for a 2.00 average. Then in the first National Hockey League playoff ever, he blanked Ottawa, 1-0, then beat them, 4-2, to take the Canadiens into the Stanley Cup final. Two teams from the Western and Pacific Leagues challenged that year, but Vezina and his teammates weren't fazed at all. They whipped Vancouver, 3-2 and 2-1, then toppled Calgary, 6-1, and 3-0. In six playoff and Stanley Cup games, the great Vezina allowed just six goals, for a fantastic 1.00 average.

There was little talk about Vezina's possible illness the next year. He was his usual spectacular self, with a 1.9 goals-against average, although he faltered a bit in the playoffs. But when he reported to camp for the 1925–26 season, it was obvious that something was wrong. He looked drawn and weary, not the same Vezina by any means.

Vezina was a big man by goaltender's standards, a six-footer with classic good looks. And when his appearance began to change as illness overtook him, his fans could see it immediately.

Georges was very anxious to play that year because

it was the first season in which United States teams would be competing in the NHL. And conversely, hockey fans in America couldn't wait to see the legendary Frenchman in action.

The season opened in Pittsburgh on November 29, 1925, and more than 6,000 fans were on hand cheering the great Vezina as he came out on the ice. They didn't know that the goalie was suffering a 105-degree fever, and having alternating hot flashes and cold chills. Yet with Pittsburgh controlling play in the opening period, Vezina showed them what they wanted to see—the finest goaltending the NHL had yet produced. He turned away shot after shot with the same acrobatic dexterity he had shown some 15 years earlier when the Canadiens first saw him.

Then, in the dressing room between periods, Vezina suffered an arterial hemmorhage. Yet he insisted on taking to the ice for the second session. Shortly after the period began, Vezina realized he couldn't even see the flitting puck as it was passed and poked around the rink. But it was too late. Before he could call time Georges Vezina collapsed in his goal crease. He was carried from the ice.

At long last the doctors had a chance to give him a thorough examination. It was an advanced case of tuberculosis, and there was nothing they could do. Vezina went home to his native Chicoutimi to await the inevitable. And there, on March 24, 1926, the handsome Frenchman died. Just the week before, the Canadiens had been eliminated from the playoffs for the first time in years.

Needless to say, Vezina's funeral was a cause for national mourning. He was one of the first great hockey heroes and his death shocked the nation. A year later the Vezina Trophy was created in his honor. It has been given to the league's best goaltender every year since.

If Georges Vezina represented the calm competitiveness of one side of hockey, Howie Morenz was the fire and brimstone that has characterized so many of the game's superstars. Morenz, in fact, can be classified as the NHL's first superstar, since he came along just when the league was getting started and expanding into the United States.

Most people will say that hockey is a faster game today than it was in the old days. Fresh lines come onto the ice every two minutes or so, and the players can go full tilt. When Joe Malone scored 44 goals in 20 games back in 1918, he was on the ice for about 50 of the 60 minutes each night. "I should have scored more, playing that much," Malone would say in later years.

But any discussion of speed begins and ends with Howie Morenz. When he came along he brought a new definition of the word with him.

Morenz may have been the most idolized player in Montreal Canadien history. Fans at the old Forum would rise to their feet every time old number 7 picked up the puck behind his own net and began one of his famous rushes up ice.

He moved like a blur, carrying the puck as if it were part of his body, attached directly to the stick. He went around or through rival defensemen until he got into position, and then, fired the puck like a bullet into opposing nets.

Veteran hockey man King Clancy never forgot the sight of Morenz rushing up ice. Recalling Howie in later years, Clancy compared him with some of the other great scorers of the game: "I've seen 'em all score.

There was Gordie Howe, knocking everyone over with his windshield-wiper elbows, Rocket Richard, coming down with that mad look on his face, guys hanging all over him. And Hull, booming that slapshot from anywhere on the ice. But let me tell you . . . I never saw anybody score like Morenz on a furious rush down center ice." And Elmer Ferguson, a veteran hockey writer who had seen them all, once said: "When Morenz skated full speed, everyone else on the ice seemed to be skating backward."

Strangely enough, the idol of all Canada, the man who typified the Montreal Canadiens, the Flying Frenchmen, didn't have a single ounce of French blood in him. He was of German and Swiss descent. Yet for Montreal fans, it didn't matter. Morenz was one of them and they took him to their hearts from the first.

Howie Morenz was born in Mitchell, Ontario, a hamlet near Stratford, a much larger town. It was there that young Howie played as a youth and acquired his nickname, "The Stratford Streak."

Howie's father worked on the railroad and wasn't home very much, but it didn't stop the youngster from learning to play hockey at an early age. Nothing really stopped Canadian kids from learning their sport. When Howie was still a youngster, he often played with boys much older because of his skating ability, and he took tremendous beatings from these youths. Many times he'd return home battered from combat and tell his parents he wasn't going to play anymore. Yet as soon as the wounds healed, Howie was back out there. The game was already in his blood.

Montreal Canadien boss Leo Dandurand was in the stands one night as Howie played with the amateur Stratford team. Howie was all over the ice . . . skating, checking, shooting, scoring, and making opposing defensemen look foolish. Dandurand dispatched his aide, Cecil Hart, to make an offer. Howie was already working with his father on the railroad and at first he didn't want to leave. Mr. Morenz left the decision to his son. Howie accepted. Then he got a case of the jitters, changed his mind, returned the check and contract, and left the Canadiens. It took a personal visit from Dandurand and Hart to convince Morenz that hockey was really what he wanted.

Howie arrived on the Montreal scene at the outset of the 1923–1924 season. He was treated roughly by the veteran players who tried to intimidate him. But his natural talents soon prevailed and before the season ended he was leading the Canadiens to a Stanley Cup triumph.

That was the beginning of the Morenz legend. He lived as he played—fast—and there are stories of Howie going for a night on the town and coming back to play sensational hockey the following afternoon. Once he spent an entire afternoon at newsman Elmer Ferguson's house, drinking beer and eating limburger cheese and onions. Ferguson flatly told him he'd never be able to play that night.

Morenz just laughed. That night he scored three goals and made it look easy. Howie Morenz could do no wrong.

He scored 13 goals his rookie year (remember the 24-game schedule), good enough for a seventh-place tie in NHL scoring. He could dish it out as well as take it, but right from his rookie year he played a clean game of hockey, staying away from the numerous stick fights and brutal clashes that characterized the game then.

By his second year, Morenz was a superstar, quickly

gaining a reputation not only as a scorer, but as a fine two-way player (offense and defense) as well.

Conn Smythe, the founder of the Toronto Maple Leafs, said that Morenz made one of the greatest plays he'd ever seen against the Boston Bruins. With a typical quick rush, Howie was hurrying the puck up ice. Tough Eddie Shore and another Bruin defenseman came at him from opposite directions. At the last second, Howie actually leaped off the ice and burst through them. Another Bruin swooped up and Howie fired his shot from about 25 feet out. It missed, caroming off the boards all the way back to Shore at the blue line. Shore, himself a fast skater, broke up ice and caught the entire Canadien team sleeping. He was all alone and was going in unopposed.

But Morenz never stopped moving. After taking his shot, he leaped again to give himself more speed swinging around the goal cage, then he came out flying in pursuit of Shore. Somehow he caught Shore as Eddie bore in on the Montreal goal. Morenz actually skated *around* Shore and took the puck away from the bewildered defenseman. Then, without a moment's pause, Howie began a rush of his own back up ice.

"I couldn't believe it," recalled Conn Smythe. "My mouth just dropped open. Morenz went from the net to the blue line faster than I could say 'blue line.' I was awed by the play. Actually, Morenz was doing what he did to me for years. The man just took my breath away."

Morenz was a fiery competitor as well as a spectacular player. He hated to lose, and would often brood after a defeat, especially if he felt he could have done something to change the outcome. Yet his desire to win imbued the entire Canadien team with a spirit that lives on with Les Canadiens today. In addition, it's often been said that the flamboyant lifestyle and play of Morenz was one of the prime reasons that hockey franchises from the United States entered the National Hockey League from 1924 to 1926. With a drawing card like Morenz, hockey was assured of ticket-buyers in the new cities and new country.

Morenz continued to be the NHL's ranking superstar throughout the 1920's. Although the shorter schedule didn't allow for the big point totals we see today, Howie got his share. He scored 30 goals in 30 games during the 1924–25 season, and you can't get much better than that. He led the league in scoring with 33 goals and 18 assists for 51 points in 43 games during 1927–28, then did it again with 28 goals and 23 assists for another 51 in 1930–31.

He won the Hart Trophy as the league's Most Valuable Player in 1928, 1931, and again in 1932. But the rest of the Morenz saga is a tragic one. During the 1933–34 season, Howie scored just eight goals in 39 games. He was no longer the flashy scorer of earlier years. It's hard to say whether his decline resulted from a natural erosion or from too much fast living, but Canadien owners realized they had to make a move, do what they believed best for the franchise.

Howie himself was despondent over the booing that was beginning to come down from the stands. In his lowest moods he talked of being traded, but no one really expected it to happen. Then, just before the 1934–35 season, Leo Dandurand announced that Howie Morenz had been traded to the Chicago Black Hawks.

Some say the trade finished Morenz, that it broke his heart. He had been the most popular player in Montreal history for 11 years, and suddenly he was gone. Canadien officials were equally dismayed by the ending of an era. They vowed immediately that Howie's number, 7, would never again be worn by a Montreal player. And it hasn't been, right to this day.

As for Morenz, he was obviously unhappy in Chicago. He played well at times, and even scored against his old mates in the final game of the year at the Forum. He received a standing ovation from the fans who knew him so well, and tears came into his eyes. But the next season he was shipped to the New York Rangers, and his play deteriorated further.

Then, prior to the 1936–37 season, Howie was suddenly and unexpectedly traded back to Montreal! It was a second lease on life for him. He no longer had the blazing speed, but playing in the Forum once more he often executed one of his unique, scintillating rushes. On the night of January 28, 1937, Howie was carrying the puck against Chicago when he was checked hard and went into the boards feet first. As his skate hit the boards, Howie's leg snapped with a sharp sound that could be heard all over the ice. The onetime superstar lay on the ice in excruciating pain.

In the hospital Howie Morenz realized for the first time that his hockey career might be over. What happened in the ensuing weeks is hazy. It is said that Howie fretted so much that he suffered a nervous breakdown. Then, on top of that, he developed heart trouble. Scores of people visited him at the hospital, yet his condition worsened. In early March, he appeared better. Then on March 8, 1937, the 36-year-old Morenz got out of bed, took two steps, and crumpled to the floor—dead. An embolism had stopped his heart.

The funeral was held at center ice at the Forum. Thousands filed past the casket of their fallen idol, as an era in National Hockey League history came to a sad finale.

Vezina the cool one, Morenz the competitor, and now Shore the brawler. That was Eddie Shore, a rock-ribbed defenseman for the Boston Bruins who typified still another side of early hockey . . . the roughness and brutality that had been part of the game since its inception.

Eddie Shore was tough from the start. He came out of the western Canadian prairie where as a youngster he labored on his family's farm in Saskatchewan. He tamed wild horses and took care of cattle, doing many jobs that most grown men would find too demanding. By the time he reached his late teens he was lean and hard, and raring to go.

Despite his many hours on the farm, Shore spent just as much time on the ice. He was the star of every league he played in from the first and he played with a determination that no man should be better than he was. He worked hard at his game, driving himself and striving for perfection every step of the way.

By 1926 Shore was in the National Hockey League, playing defense for the Boston Bruins. And it wasn't long before he proved to be an extraordinary man with extraordinary talents. Judged on individual skills alone, Shore was a great player. But he came into the league with something else as well.

Eddie Shore had a spirit, an inner drive that manifested itself in many ways, some of them quite startling. He fought and feuded with opponents, squabbled with fans and the press, and remained a controversial figure even though he won four Most Valuable Player awards and was chosen to the all-star team many times.

Howie Morenz was on the wane as a hockey idol by 1930, and that's when Shore was coming into his own. He was the big draw in the '30's, and helped make hockey one of the major sports in the United States.

And he also helped bring the NHL to even greater popularity in Canada, where junior and amateur hockey were still potential rivals.

Shore on the ice was like an accident looking for a place to happen. He defied his opponents to get him and took a tremendous amount of punishment from those who tried. During the course of his NHL career, Shore had an estimated 900 stitches on his face and body; sustained fractures of the back, hip, and collarbone; had every single tooth in his mouth knocked out; had his nose broken 14 times, and his jaw five times.

Yet Eddie Shore stayed in the game if it was humanly possible and sometimes when those around thought it wasn't. And he always played well.

Defensemen played strictly defense in the old days. There was an unwritten rule that a backliner never crossed his own blue line, even when starting a rush. He'd dump the puck to his forwards and then hang back to prevent his opponents from getting the offensive advantage.

Not Shore. He broke the rules. When he started a rush with his long strides and great skating ability, he didn't stop. He could shoot the puck like a forward . . . in fact, he could do everything a forward could do, and sometimes more. Though the stats don't sound like much until you remember the shorter schedule, Shore racked up 12 goals and seven assists for 19 points during the 1928–29 season. That placed him sixth in the entire American Division of the NHL.

Yet Shore also excelled as a defender. He had all the slick moves, pokechecking and hookchecking with the best of them. And, of course, he never hesitated to use his body to stop a play. But some people tend to forget all this. When they think of Eddie Shore, they think first, last, and always about his classic, brutal confrontations on the ice.

There was one incident in Boston during the 1933–34 season that might well have ended in a real tragedy. The Bruins were going against the Toronto Maple Leafs when Eddie, in a personal slump, had the puck stolen by King Clancy.

Shore fell to the ice, got up, and took off with mayhem in his eye. He spotted two Leaf players, Ace Bailey and Red Horner, and took a rush at them. To this day, some observers feel that Shore mistook Bailey for Clancy. Anyway, Eddie lowered his shoulder and cracked into Bailey's lower back. The Leaf player flipped over backwards and struck his head on the ice. He was unconscious on contact. The injury looked serious.

But it wasn't over yet. Red Horner, who had been near Bailey on the ice, thought he saw Shore smiling. He skated over and rapped Eddie with a roundhouse sucker-punch.

Now Shore went down, and it was his head that hit first, the blood gushing from a wide-open wound almost immediately. Both players, Bailey and Shore, were carried from the ice as the crowd fell silent.

Shore recovered slowly and finally returned to action, but for a while, doctors feared for Bailey's life. The Leafs went so far as to make funeral arrangements for their player. But the defenseman also recovered, though he never played hockey again. A few years later Shore and Bailey shook hands at center ice during an old-timers game. There didn't seem to be any hard feelings.

At any rate, the incident didn't slow Shore down. He played with the same recklessness as before. He was involved in another major ice collision that saw his left ear almost cut off. The first doctors to examine it didn't think they could save it. Shore would have none of that.

"I found a doctor who said he could save the ear," recalls Shore. "When he asked me what kind of anesthetic I wanted, I told him to give me a mirror so I could watch the way he sewed me up. I told him I was a simple farmboy who didn't want his looks fouled up. And you know, I made him change the last stitch, otherwise it would have left a scar."

Such was Shore. There was still another incident that showed the single-mindedness of this rugged individual from Saskatchewan. It happened in January of 1929. The Bruins were slated to play the Montreal Maroons in Montreal, and as was the custom then, the team left Boston by train the day before. At the station, everyone looked for Shore. He wasn't around. It was time for the train to leave, and it did.

The Bruin management couldn't figure out what had happened to their star. He was always prompt. They didn't know that Eddie had become involved in a huge traffic tieup in Boston and had arrived at the station just as the last car was pulling out. Desperate, Eddie looked for another means of transportation.

There was none. A bad sleet storm and blizzard had caused cancellation of all air traffic. No other trains were scheduled to leave. Shore called some of his friends and one finally volunteered to lend the hockey star his limousine and chauffeur. The man picked up Eddie at 11:30 P.M. and the two started the 350-mile drive to Montreal along New England roads that in no way resembled the superhighways of today. Furthermore, the storm was rapidly worsening.

With the weather so bad, the chauffeur set out at a snail's pace. Finally, the impatient Shore took the wheel. He found an all-night gas station, bought chains, and continued into the teeth of the blizzard.

When the ice froze the one windshield wiper, Shore removed the top half of the windshield and kept driving, the icy wind and hail blowing fiercely in his face. By 5 A.M., Shore and the frightened chauffeur were moving across the mountains of New Hampshire. Then the chains began giving. Just as it looked as if the trip must end, Shore found another remote service station, got gas, and bought another set of chains.

By 3 P.M. the next day, Shore was exhausted. He gave the wheel back to the chauffeur, but as soon as Eddie fell asleep, the other man ran the car into a ditch. Shore awoke, hiked a mile to a farmhouse, rented a team of horses and dragged the car out.

At 5:30 P.M., Shore drove up to the Windsor Hotel in Montreal. Art Ross, manager of the Bruins, recalls the sight of Shore coming into the hotel lobby after his drive.

"The man was in bad shape, certainly in no condition to play hockey," said Ross. "His face was puffy from windburn and frostbite. His eyes were completely bloodshot and his fingers were bent like claws from gripping the steering wheel. And his legs were so stiff from hitting the brake and clutch that he couldn't walk a straight line. He insisted on playing and I tried to talk him out of it. He wouldn't budge. So I told him he could suit up, but I still didn't plan to use him."

Once the game started, Ross changed his mind. It was a tough, fast game and he wanted to win it. That meant using Eddie Shore. When he got in the game, Shore looked like anything but a tired man. He stopped the Maroon rushes and slammed Hooley Smith to the ice, drawing the game's first penalty.

Midway through the second period he grabbed the

puck behind his own net and began one of his patented rushes up the ice. He swerved and faked, finally breaking past the last Maroon defender and firing a bullet into the lower corner of the net.

Shore was on the ice during the entire third period and helped his team hang onto the 1-0 lead he had given them. When it was over, local writers, hearing of Eddie's ordeal just to get to Montreal, called his performance one of the most inspired of all time. And indeed it was.

As his playing career neared an end, Shore made plans to remain in hockey. Soon after retiring in 1940, he bought the Springfield team of the American League, running the entire operation, from front office to coach. And he was as controversial in his new job as he had been in his old.

He feuded with everyone, even some of his own players. During the almost 30 years that he ran the club, Shore suffered four near-fatal heart attacks, yet he practiced faithfully with his team every day, ignoring the advice of doctors and friends alike.

He was a devout student of his sport. He tried to control everything his players did, including the way they held their sticks and their skating styles, right down to the distance between their skates as they glided up and down the ice. And the incident that prompted Shore to give up the team was a players' strike in 1967. Whom were they striking against? Why Shore, of course, and some of his unorthodox tactics.

Some of the things he made his players do were bizarre. Yet Eddie firmly believed that he was making them into better hockey players. Over the years he had his charges tap dance in a hotel lobby, taped their hands to their sticks, tied a player's skates together with rope, instructed the players' wives on how to treat their husbands during a slump. Once he even told a player that he was parting his hair on the wrong side of his head.

Another time Shore pulled his entire team off the ice in a dispute with an official. Only his goalie remained. The ref threatened to drop the puck and did, and the enemy team was so bewildered that they all botched the first shot. Somehow, the goalie managed to stop three others, point blank, before falling on the puck. Only then did Shore return his skaters to the ice.

Yet he had his boosters. NHL defenseman Kent Douglas, a rough customer himself, played for Shore at Springfield and held the old tough-guy in awe.

"Playing for Shore is like getting a doctorate in hockey science," Douglas maintained. "He taught me things about the game that no one else ever thought about. For instance, he showed me that you don't always have to hit a man real hard. Sometimes you just have to get a piece of him to get the job done. And no one knew how to maneuver a man until he was off balance like Eddie. Balance was everything to Eddie. If you had it and the other guy didn't, you could wipe him out."

In one sense, Shore was undoubtedly a hockey genius. But geniuses always have a way of bordering on the eccentric. For Eddie Shore, that kind of behavior was a way of life. Yet he once told a reporter that he wasn't sorry for a single thing he'd done during his long career. And there was little doubt in anyone's mind that Eddie Shore meant what he said. That's just the way he was.

Many other stars shone in hockey's infancy and the early years of the NHL, many of them still legends today. Yet in Vezina, Morenz, and Shore there lies the whole essence of the game as it was played between 1910 and 1940. So alike, although so different were these three men. Each was a superstar, each a hero. And each helped to build the sport he loved.

Vezina was an athlete with class, a gentleman who played a clean, but hard game. That same style is alive today in players like Jean Ratelle and, in past years, Jean Beliveau.

Morenz was the fiery competitor, a hell-for-leather type with a burning desire to win. Rocket Richard followed that tradition at Montreal and traces of the same spirit flow in the veins of Bobby Orr, Gil Perrault, and Phil Esposito.

Shore was the badman, the villain, who just happened to have a world of talent to boot. Young Stan Mikita was such a player (though he has mellowed in later years) and Brad Park has shown some of the same characteristics.

So the bloodlines from the past continue. There were so many more pioneers, so many great stories that it would be impossible to include them all here. Ice hockey has a folksy kind of history, perhaps more so than any other major sport and that's because of the players and their unique backgrounds and origins.

In many ways, the hockey player of those days was a different breed of cat. The game was different. Schedules were shorter, there wasn't as much travel, yet the player himself was an iron man, staying on the ice for almost the entire 60 minutes. That wasn't easy.

Those men who chose to make the ice sport their life seem to have had a special determination, a burning desire all their own. And sometimes they seemed fully capable of miracles. Here's one example.

On April 7, 1928, the New York Rangers were facing the Montreal Maroons in the best of five Stanley

Cup final series. The New Yorkers were already trailing by a game and had to win this one to get back in the series. It was a scoreless tie midway through the second period. Then Montreal's Nels Stewart fired a backhander at New York goalie Lorne Chabot.

The shot conked Chabot on the head and he was carried from the ice and taken to the hospital for treatment of an eye injury. In those days, teams carried just one goaltender who kept playing, no matter what. It was a rare instance when a goalie couldn't continue, but it happened to the Rangers on that April night.

New York coach Lester Patrick, a 44-year-old hockey veteran, asked the Maroons if he could suit up Alex Connell, an Ottawa goalie who happened to be at the game. The Maroon management said no. Patrick then spied another net-minder in the crowd and asked permission to use him. Again the Maroons said no.

Patrick started to burn. He could see the Maroons were trying to squeeze him into a corner. He looked at his disconsolate team. Suddenly he turned about four shades of crimson and blurted out:

"The hell with them. I'll play goal myself!"

His players couldn't believe it. Patrick had never been a great hockey player. He and his brother Frank were better known as organizers, men who put big-time hockey on the map in western Canada, then later in the United States. Now, at age 44, he was ready to take on what has been described as the most nerve-shattering job in all sports.

But Lester meant what he said. Before anyone could utter a word, he was pulling on Chabot's gear, none of which fit him very well.

"I'll worry about stopping the pucks, you worry about getting the rebounds," he told his club as they returned to the ice. The Maroons licked their chops.

They figured it would be duck soup against the old man.

In the final few minutes of the second period, Lester Patrick somehow stopped the first few shots the Montrealers fired at him. Then the session ended. Patrick's performance had given his mates heart, and Bill Cook of the Rangers broke the ice early in the final period, scoring on a long slapshot and giving the Rangers a 1-0 lead. Several minutes later Nels Stewart finally beat Patrick after being stopped on several hard shots. That made it 1-1, but the Maroons couldn't score again, as Patrick made several difficult saves, difficult for a regular goalie, unbelievable for him.

The game went into overtime and after some seven minutes, the Rangers' Frank Boucher drove home the winning goal. Somehow, Patrick and the Rangers had done it.

Patrick's performance received the plaudits of hockey fans everywhere. He had stopped 15 or more tough Montreal shots, and had shut off the Maroons on three power plays. It was an incredible performance. But Lester Patrick didn't want to press his luck. He found a suitable replacement for the injured Chabot and the Rangers went on to take the Cup in five games. It had surely been the inspired performance of Lester Patrick that turned the tide.

Lester Patrick's feat is one of the many hockey legends that have carried down through the years. It's been the Lester Patricks, as well as the Vezinas, the Morenzes, and the Shores who have brought the game from the lakes and ponds of the Canadian wilds into the plush, modern arenas where it's played today. And they did it with the qualities that make the men and their sport unique, and very great.

3   *The Growing Years*

BETWEEN 1935 AND 1942, the National Hockey League was in the process of finding itself. The league had grown to ten teams as early as 1926, but there were still many unstable franchises, and changes occurred frequently during the ensuing years.

When the Montreal Maroons dropped out of the league in 1938, the NHL was reduced to just seven teams. The final dropout occurred four years later when the Brooklyn Americans (formerly the New York Americans) withdrew. This left six teams—the Montreal Canadiens, Toronto Maple Leafs, Boston Bruins, New York Rangers, Chicago Black Hawks, and Detroit Red Wings.

That was the National Hockey League for the next 25 years, a six-team loop in which the best players in the world competed. It seems as if the sport did not have enough backing to support additional franchises, but these six were solid and had their own groups of fans. The two Canadian cities, of course, had no problem, except perhaps finding enough seats for their fans.

And the sport had become well enough established in the four large American cities that held franchises to assure continued success.

At Stanley Cup time, the top four teams entered the playoffs, the first-place finisher facing number three, and the second-place team meeting the fourth best. The two winners would clash for the Cup, giving two thirds of the league a shot at hockey's top prize each year.

So the NHL had worked out a nice, neat way of doing things and it survived on this setup for more than two decades. In fact, by 1949, the league was on a 70-game schedule and sneaking right up on the modern age.

Hockey in the late '40's, the '50's, and early '60's was a remarkably solid proposition. Solid in that the play was tight and consistent. Each team dressed fewer than 20 players for a game, and there were only six teams, so that less than 120 men were National Hockey League players. And since every town throughout Canada worked to develop hockey players, the NHL was one of the tightest-knit fraternities in the world. The players were surely the best.

Those who frown on the proliferation of teams today will point to the old six-team NHL and claim the brand of hockey was much better then because only the cream of the crop got to be pros. There may be some truth in that. On the other hand, many players who might have blossomed as pros surely languished in the minor leagues for want of a place to play.

That wasn't all. Hockey players also have a tradition of staying in the game as long as they possibly can. That's how much they love it. But with a six-team league, veteran players were forced out of the game sooner by eager young talent ready to take their place. That's why during the '50's and early '60's, hockey fans scanning minor-league rosters would be amazed at the number of NHL veterans hanging on for a few more years, a few more goals, and a lot more pounding.

There was little chance of their ever getting back to the NHL, but they took the good with the bad and continued playing. For many, it was the only thing they knew. They had been victims of the old "letter of intent" system where they'd been bound to their hockey clubs since the age of fourteen or so. From that point in their lives, everything was hockey. Education and preparation for a trade was put in the background. And with just a few spots in the NHL available each year, one wonders what happened to the players who didn't manage to find a berth.

That was and is the beauty of expansion. It gives more hockey players a chance. When the league first expanded in 1967, there was a tremendous influx of these veteran players from the minors. It was good for everyone. The players got another shot at the big time, and loyal fans had the chance to see old favorites in action again. And, from a practical point of view, there was more money available to the veterans, giving them a better chance to build a future.

But before going into the specifics of the most ambitious expansion program ever undertaken by a major sport, let's go back to the game of that post-war period, and look at some of the super-players who dominated the six-team National Hockey League.

The decade of the '40's began in a scramble, with the league finally settling into its new pattern. But then came the war, and just as in the first World War, many Canadian players donned the uniform of their country and NHL rosters once again fell into a state of constant flux.

At the end of the war in 1945, a sort of normalcy

returned, but it was one of those periods in which many veteran players were reaching the end of the line, and new, young talents were coming up to replace them.

There was one major change in the game, the inclusion of a center line, or red line, on the ice which further restricted the wide-open forward pass and made the game a little tighter. The postwar era also saw an end to the dominance of the American clubs, which had taken seven of eight Stanley Cups from 1935 to 1943. The balance of power now moved back north, where Montreal and Toronto were building big winners.

More fans than ever began turning out at hockey games, and the Stanley Cup playoffs were taking on special meaning in the United States, beginning to be viewed with the same enthusiasm that greeted the World Series and National Football League championship game.

As in the past, the players had a magnetism, a color all their own. Players who operated on the same forward line had a double identity, both as individuals and as a line. Fans didn't have to be told about the "Kraut Line," the "Punch Line," or the "Production Line." They knew exactly what those words meant and all about the players involved. That tradition carries on today, with the Rangers' Ratelle-Hadfield-Gilbert forming the "GAG Line" (goal-a-game) and Buffalo's youngsters Perreault-Robert-Martin making up the "French Connection." When lines like these stay together for years, they invariably pick up legions of fans.

But when you think of a single player, one man who typified hockey during the postwar days, the name of Maurice "Rocket" Richard invariably comes to mind. In a sense, the Rocket was the Babe Ruth of Hockey, exploding onto the scene with an abundance of spectacular goals. He was the man who put the puck in the net in a dynamic way, the clutch player who got the score when it was needed most.

The Rocket netted some 544 goals during his 18-year career with the Montreal Canadiens, and gathered another 82 in Stanley Cup play. His totals are only surpassed by the great Gordie Howe and the spectacular Bobby Hull. But that hardly mattered to Richard fans. To them the Rocket was the main man.

It wasn't hard to see why fans in Montreal took Richard to heart almost immediately. He was the closest thing to Howie Morenz since Howie Morenz. The Rocket was a talented skater who loved rushing the puck up ice. And when he saw goaldust, he got a wild-eyed determination that fans could never forget. He wanted that score and had the knack of working his way in close and getting it. Or he could pull up short and fire a low, hard, accurate shot that left goalies shell-shocked.

Furthermore, and in this he differed from Morenz, the Rocket had a temper that could flare at any time. No one pushed him around and got away with it. He'd push back, sometimes pushing the wrong people at the wrong time. It often got him in trouble, yet endeared him even more to his thousands of fans.

"But Richard is not the Pope," protested a publicity writer when he saw the idolatry in which the Rocket was held.

"No," answered his companion, Frank Selke, who was once managing director of the team, "He is God."

Maurice Richard was born in the Bordeaux section of Montreal at about the same time Howie Morenz was first playing for the Canadiens. The Rocket's dad, Onesime Richard, was a semi-pro hockey star who bought his son a pair of skates when Maurice was just four. The Rocket got a lot of use out of them. "The winters were extremely cold when I was a youngster in the twenties," he says. "There weren't very many cars out and we used to actually skate to school and back right on the frozen streets. We did it from about December to February."

It wasn't long before the young Rocket was playing hockey on the frozen rivers and lakes around his home.

"If a fellow really put his mind to it, he could play all the hockey he wanted," Maurice recalled. "I put my mind to it."

So began the development of a hockey superstar. The Rocket says that when he reached his early teens he still had no plans to be a professional because he wasn't that good. Well, he got good in a hurry, good enough to play with some top amateur and minor league teams before he was out of his teens. A broken ankle and broken wrist hampered his progress, but that was only a temporary delay. The Rocket was coming.

He arrived on the Montreal scene in the fall of 1942. He may have had an advantage because some of the players were already away at the War. But it wasn't long before the Rocket's great talent shone through. He made the team and played in 16 games before injury struck—Richard suffered a broken ankle.

The next season, things started coming together. The Rocket was put on a line with center Elmer Lach and left wing Toe Blake. The trio clicked almost from the start. The line was instrumental in leading the Canadiens to the league title and a sweep of Chicago in the Stanley Cup final round. The Rocket, in his first full season, scored 32 goals and picked up 22 assists. In the playoffs, he showed the hockey world that he was the game's next superstar, ramming home 12 goals (a record at that time) and picking up five assists in just nine games.

But the best was yet to come. It happened the very next year, the Rocket's third in the league. Though hampered by a nagging knee injury, Richard continued to score goals in his own blazing style. It seemed as if every night he was getting another. In fact, by the time he had played 25 of the team's 50 games, the Rocket had 26 goals, and fans began wondering how long his goal-a-game pace would last.

It lasted, all right. In the 50th and final game of the year, Richard blasted down his right wing, cut over the middle, and jammed the puck home from in close, his 50th goal in 50 games. The total was a new National Hockey League record then, an almost unheard of feat. Joe Malone had once scored 44 goals in 20 games, but that was in the early days. Under modern rules, no one thought a 50-goal season possible. But the Rocket did it.

Yet Rocket Richard was more than a prolific goal scorer. He put the puck in the net with a kind of dynamic verve, and explosiveness that was likely to erupt at any given moment. Fans loved him for that and they loved him as much for a personality that matched his stickwork. The Rocket was a Frenchman all the way. He spoke nary a word of English when he came into the NHL and the language came to him slowly. But he never had any problems expressing himself on the ice.

The Canadiens were playing the Rangers one night at Madison Square Garden in New York. Ranger defenseman Bob Dill was getting on the Rocket, giving him a going over whenever he had a chance, and hoping to deter the great Frenchman's scoring thrusts. Finally the two tangled behind the New York net and Dill began screaming at Richard.

"He called me a French so-and-so," recalls the Rocket, "and that set me off."

The two began trading punches and Rocket dropped Dill with a pair of rights. Dill got up and tried again, with the same result. Then the ref sent both players to the penalty box and sure enough, Dill jumped at Richard once more.

"When I floored him in the penalty box, that finished it," said the Rocket.

Incidents such as that served notice that Richard couldn't be intimidated. It had to be that way, or every tough guy in the league would be taking pot shots at him. After the game, the Rocket saw Dill outside the Garden and invited him to dinner. Such is the nature of the sport.

There are two different worlds on and off the ice. Rocket himself once said that, "Players in the NHL live by the jungle code. You have to make do in the best way you know how."

Each player had little tricks he used, things not quite legal but that he could usually get away with to help his game. The Rocket admitted using his left hand to hold off opponents who were trying to check him closely. This kept the defenseman or checker from effectively reaching for the puck. Yet in spite of his occasional flareups, the Rocket welcomed rough play.

"I liked it when someone on the other team checked me closely, because it made me work harder. If a guy was sticking close to me I really wanted to get away from him and that made me try even more to get my goals. If no one was on my back and I was always left alone, I don't think I would have accomplished what I did during my career.

"Sure, I got nailed once in a while. But when I'd get put into the boards real hard or tripped up, I'd usually get mad and retaliate. But for the most part it worked out well and I've really got no complaints about the caliber of play."

The caliber of Rocket's play continued high. The Canadiens were tough again and he continued to score goals. On October 29, 1952, the Canadiens came into Maple Leaf Gardens in Toronto with the Rocket just two goals shy of Nels Stewart's all-time record of 324 goals. A capacity crowd jammed the arena to see if the Rocket could become the all-time goal-getter that night. Sure enough, he wasted no time, banging home the needed goals within the first six minutes of the game.

In another game against the Leafs, the Rocket scored all five goals in a 5-1 Montreal victory. The Rocket will never forget that game, and for a good reason. At the end of every hockey game, a sports writer picks the night's "Three Stars." The general pattern usually finds two players from the winning team and one from the losing club. That night in Toronto it was announced that all three stars were going to Rocket Richard.

But perhaps the most dramatic incident in the Rocket's stormy career occurred in March 1955. As background, two facts are important. First, despite his great goal-scoring over the years, the Rocket had never taken the overall point title in the NHL, a crown that goes to the player with the most combined goals and assists, each worth a point. He had missed by a single point on several occasions and was always near the top. In 1955, it looked as if he might make it. The Rocket himself wanted it and so did his fans. Passionately.

The second point to remember is that Rocket had never gotten along particularly well with NHL President Clarence Campbell. In fact, during the 1946–47 Stanley Cup playoffs, Richard became embroiled in a violent clash with Toronto's Bill Ezinicki and Vic Lynn. After the game he was notified that Campbell had suspended him for a brief period. There had been bad blood between the two ever since.

Now we can go back to that March game with the Boston Bruins. Coming into the the contest, the Rocket led teammate Bernie "Boom Boom" Geoffrion by four points in the scoring race. There were four games left, and it looked as if Richard would finally get that elusive scoring title.

In the Bruin game, Rocket was having a bad time with Hal Laycoe. Finally, the two began going at it and the Rocket used his stick to work on Laycoe's face. When linesman Cliff Thompson tried to intervene, the Richard temper was still at a high point and Rocket slugged the linesman. Pretty soon both teams were battling in one of hockey's classic slugfests.

The next day Campbell assessed the situation. He didn't want that type of mayhem to blacken the reputation of the league and he took radical action. He suspended the Rocket for the remaining games of the regular season and for the entire Stanley Cup playoff. The news hit Montreal like an atomic bomb.

Several days later the Canadiens hosted the Red Wings at the Forum. Rocket knew trouble was coming.

"I was numb when I heard the news of the suspension," he recalls. "Maybe for the final three games of the season, but never for the playoffs. That wasn't right. When I got home I began getting phone calls from fans. All of them were threatening trouble, telling me they were going to get Campbell and really cause trouble. They sounded serious and I tried to stop them, but they wouldn't listen."

The game with the Wings started calmly enough, though the fans were booing Geoffrion every time he stepped on the ice. They didn't want him to catch the Rocket in scoring.

"What could I do?" he said later. "I couldn't stop trying." Sure enough, the Boomer scored five points in the last three games to take the scoring title by a point, 75-74. Then, as both clubs skated up and down the ice trying to forget the suspension and threats, a loud bang sounded in the Forum, followed by a pungent, stinging aroma. Someone had set off a tear gas bomb.

The game was immediately forfeited to the Red Wings, who were leading, 4-1, but that wasn't the end of it. In a show of defiance, Campbell himself had come to the game and had to be protected by a cordon of police as the angry fans peppered him with eggs, fruit, bottles, and anything they could get their hands on. When the Forum was cleared after the tear gas, the angry fans took to the streets.

There were an estimated 10,000 fans hanging around the Forum, chanting things like, "Kill Campbell!" Suddenly some people began throwing rocks at the windows of passing cars. Cab drivers were pulled from their vehicles and beaten, while their cars were overturned. People threw bricks through the windows of the Forum and nearby stores. The suspension of the Rocket had precipitated a full-scale riot.

The police were called out in droves but had a hard time controlling the mob as it moved into Montreal's business district, continuing to smash windows and cause wholesale destruction. Then store looting began.

When it ended some six hours later, there was an estimated $100,000 worth of damage to stores and property. Some 12 policemen and 25 citizens were injured and about 70 people were arrested. The police took those apprehended to central police headquarters, where they were still high with emotion. One policeman couldn't believe it. Here were some 70 citizens of Montreal under arrest and what were they talking about? Hockey! Where else could it happen?

Most of the rioters were contrite. One young man had walked up to Campbell before the tear gas bomb and squashed two tomatoes on the President's chest. He had never been in trouble before and when he came before the judge he summed up many people's feelings about the riots.

"I really didn't have anything against Campbell," the young man said. "But when I saw him at the game I just started getting angry all over again about Richard's suspension. After all, Campbell was crucifying our hero!"

And the fans of Montreal took the tomato squasher to heart, sending him all kinds of gifts and letters. He was even named the "star" of the game by a Montreal sportswriter.

The people of Montreal regretted the incident and no more trouble was expected, yet city officials thought it best if the Rocket took to the air waves and tried to maintain the calming atmosphere.

"Do no more harm," he begged his fans. "Just get behind the team in the playoffs. I will take my punishment and come back next year and help us win the Cup."

The Rocket's message proved prophetic. With their

top goal-getter sidelined, the Canadiens lost the Cup final that year to the Red Wings. But they came back the next year and for four more years after that, winning five straight Cups, a team record, and it was the Rocket, in body and spirit, who led the way.

Other great players came to the Canadiens in those years, men like Jacques Plante, Jean Beliveau, Dickie Moore, Claude Provost, Bert Olmstead, and Henri Richard, the Rocket's little brother who became known as the Pocket Rocket. Richard, Geoffrion, defensemen Doug Harvey and Tom Johnson, plus other valuable holdovers combined to give the club a balance and depth that it had lacked in some previous seasons. It was a great team, as the five Stanley Cup victories proved.

As the years went on, the Rocket began putting on weight. He came to training camp each year with a few more pounds tucked onto his 5' 10" frame and found it more difficult to get into top shape. He hadn't lost the scoring touch, but he was aware of the fact that he was slowing down.

"When my weight went up I became an easier mark for head-hunting defensemen," he admitted.

The Rocket wasn't kidding. As a flashing rookie he had been a lithe 160-pounder. In later years he was up around the 200-pound mark and that's quite a difference. Furthermore, like many older athletes, the Rocket was finding himself more susceptible than ever to injuries, and in the late '50's, for the first time he began to think about retiring. He hadn't led the league in goal-scoring since 1955.

Early in the 1958–59 season the Rocket suffered a severed Achilles tendon, and it put him on the shelf for almost three months. He came back at the tail end of the season, scored two goals in his first game and two in the next. In the Stanley Cup-winning playoffs he got 11 more, and his fans went wild in the knowledge that their hero had returned with his scoring touch intact.

Rocket played the next season with the tendon stiff and painful, and he had a mediocre year. When he finished that campaign, he had 544 goals, a league record, and another record 82 in Stanley Cup play, a total of more than six hundred scores. But the excess weight bothered him more than ever and he wasn't sure what to do about the 1960–61 season. He decided to come to training camp to find out.

"I surprised myself by playing very well in camp," he said. "I was scoring at a good clip, but I often found myself pressing and trying too hard, not in a good way. I'd get back to the bench after taking a turn and get dizzy. And I was constantly thinking about getting hurt. At my age I didn't need another broken bone or serious injury. I'd had my share. In the middle of training camp I made my decision.

"It wasn't easy. But I had other things to consider. For one thing, I didn't want all my old fans to see me, night after night, playing at less than my best. The same went for my boys. They were growing up, and why should they remember their old man as a heavy guy trying to keep up with the youngsters. So it was over."

But it had been a great career, lasting some 18 seasons. The Rocket was 39 when he quit. His 544 goals were a record then, and although both Gordie Howe and Bobby Hull have passed that total since, Richard fans like to cite an interesting statistic: The Rocket got his goals in just 978 regular season games. It took Howe some 1,132 games to get to number 545. Hull did it in 937 games, but the goals he picked up after

1967 (enabling him to pass Richard) included many scored against expansion teams which offered inferior competition during their first few years. So to many, the Rocket still remains the best pure goal-scorer who ever played the game.

Perhaps it was hockey writer Neil Offen who best put the Rocket in proper perspective as a hockey hero. Writing a daily column in a New York paper in 1971, Offen remarked:

"Maurice Richard was in town this week. Think about that. That's like saying Babe Ruth was over at the house, or Bill Tilden just dropped by, or, hey, did you see Johnny Weismuller yesterday?

"But still, the legend is there. The living legend. Think of Babe Ruth walking down Broadway . . . He is called The Rocket. When you talk about him, you call him The Rocket. When you talk to him, you address him as The Rocket. Would you have called Ruth George?"

So that was the Rocket. His kind passes through just once in a lifetime.

Comparing Rocket Richard and Gordie Howe is a classic pastime among hockey fans everywhere. Who was the greater player? *Richard!* bellows one fan. *Howe!* snarls the other. And then the furniture may begin to fly.

Where the Rocket was a flamboyant, magnetic personality, a charismatic figure, Howe was the NHL's quiet assassin, a deadly serious hockey player with more all-around skills than anyone else. There was nothing that Gordie Howe couldn't do in a hockey rink.

But Gordie Howe is not just a player of the past. Now Mr. Hockey is about to write another chapter to his already incredible story. When Howe retired from the National Hockey League after the 1970–71 season at the age of 43, most people thought it was over. But Gordie hadn't realized one long-standing ambition. He always wanted to play on the same team with at least one of his two teen-age sons.

Since the NHL had passed a rule prohibiting amateurs from signing until they were 20, Gordie more or less gave up on the idea . . . that is, until the World Hockey Association came along. The new league, which started during the 1972–73 season, is desperate for talent, and is signing some of the teen-agers that the NHL keeps hands off. In early 1973, the Houston team of the WHA made an offer. They wanted to sign Howe's two sons, Mark and Marty, 18 and 17 years old respectively, and they wanted Papa to come out of retirement to play with them.

Howe pondered the offer. After all, he's to be 45 at the outset of the 1973–74 season, but with a million-dollar package and his two sons awaiting him, he couldn't say no. At this writing, Gordie Howe is preparing to play hockey once more, to realize the last of his ambitions as an ice star. The experts are divided on just how good Howe will be. But with his natural strength, his ability, and his vast experience, he'll probably outplay the boys.

Certainly Gordie has been outplaying the entire NHL for years. He has played more seasons, played more games, scored more goals, picked up more assists, gained more points, played in more all-star games, won more Hart and Art Ross Trophies, and made more all-star teams than any other player in the history of the league.

Here are just a few of his statistics. Howe play the NHL for 25 seasons, beginning when he was 18 years old. In that time he scored 786 goals and picked up 1,023 assists. He was the league's Most Valuable Player (Hart Trophy) six times and won the scoring crown (Art Ross Trophy) on half a dozen occasions. In 12 of his 25 years he was picked to the league's first all-star team and on nine other occasions made the second team. That leaves just four seasons when he wasn't chosen.

Like Richard, Howe's been a right winger. One reason the Rocket was effective was that he was one of the few right wings with a left-handed shot and used this abnormality to his advantage. Howe was and remains the only player in the game who could shoot effectively *with either hand!*

Furthermore, many people claim that Gordie was the strongest man in the league. A teammate once defied any player to try to lift Gordie's stick off the ice. He said Gordie would hold it with one hand while those trying to lift it had to use two.

And there were those who said he was the meanest player in NHL hockey. That might be a matter of definition, but it was a cinch that no one, absolutely no one, ever messed with Gordie Howe once he had established himself as a superstar. And Howe was one of hockey's smoothest players. He did things so coolly and so effortlessly that you'd have to look twice to see them happen. And he used this skill to every bit of his advantage.

Vern Buffey, once one of the NHL's better referees, described the subtle ways in which Gordie Howe operated.

"You'll see Gordie tangling with some guy in one of the corners," Buffey said. "Then the puck will come out and you follow the play. A minute later you turn around and see the guy who was tangling with Howe lying on the ice. You know Howe did it, but there's no way you can prove it. The man is just so strong and tricky. He's got a dozen little moves he can make with his stick and elbow."

Sometimes Howe took more direct action. Several years ago, someone got the idea that you could stop the superscorers by assigning a "shadow" to them, that is a man who would come onto the ice whenever the superstar was on and just follow him around, trying to keep him from getting the puck and starting a rush.

The original shadow was a pesky defenseman named Bryan Watson, and the first man he shadowed by the great Bobby Hull. Hull, of course, was the NHL's ranking goal-scorer at the time, and his booming slapshots were the scourge of the league. Watson did a good job, hampering Hull's effectiveness to some degree. Bobby, though strong as a bull, isn't a fighter by nature, and he took a lot of the elbows, shoves, and holds that Watson dished out, and tried to beat him on pure merit and skating ability.

Then one day Watson's coach decided to use his player against Howe, who although a veteran, was still the hub of the Red Wings attack.

"I skated on with Howe and started shadowing him," Watson recalls, "much in the same way I did with Hull. Anyway, I couldn't have been out there more than a few minutes when we went in the corner after a puck. One of us kicked it out and as the play started up ice, I felt the blade of Howe's stick dangerously close to my eye.

"He didn't cut me. All he did was growl, 'Take off, junior,' and I did. I realized how easily the man could do me in if he felt inclined. Needless to say, we didn't use the shadow method with him again."

But Howe wasn't out to do bodily harm. There are incidents that show the other side of the man, too. One night the Wings were playing the Rangers in New York. Ranger goalie Gump Worsley dove to the ice in making a good save, but the puck dribbled away from the Gump and was sitting perilously close to his exposed face. As happened so often, Howe was the first one on the spot. Most players would have taken a big swing, hoping to drive the disk past the prone goalie for the score and not worry about Worsley's unprotected face. Howe didn't. He stopped and let the Gump reach out and cover the puck.

"Thanks, pal," said the grateful Worsley as he got to his feet.

"Listen," said Howe in return. "Before I'm through I'm gonna score some more on you and you'll stop some more on me. So I guess we're about even."

And in spite of having a hunger for goals, Gordie never failed to correct a goal judge when he was given a score erroneously. On more than one occasion he approached the scorer after being credited for a goal and told the man that a teammate had actually scored it.

Rough, tough, fair, generous—the quiet assassin. was once a yowling, helpless baby, just like anybody else. Born on March 31, 1928, in the hamlet of Floral, Saskatchewan, he was one of nine children born to Catherine and Albert Howe. When Gordie was still a youngster his family moved to Saskatoon, and there he learned to play hockey. In some ways, it wasn't a very pleasant experience, but it certainly served to toughen him up.

"The winters were unreal," Howe remembers. "The temperature would drop as low as 50 below zero and when it was 10 below we all figured it was warm.

"All I had for equipment was skates and a stick. The rest I made. I remember taking magazines and catalogs and sticking them in my socks to make shin pads. We didn't have pucks so we used tennis balls and they'd get so cold that they'd split in half. I don't know how we learned to play the game right, but we did."

Young Gordie practiced incessantly, by day and by night, sometimes not even taking his skates off long enough to eat. He knew he wanted to be a hockey player and nothing else mattered. He quit school, and, still playing hockey, took a job with a construction company. Part of his job was carrying 85-pound cement bags around, and he did it with zeal, knowing he'd need every ounce of strength to play in the National Hockey League. And his chance came sooner than he thought.

It was in 1943, when he was just fifteen years old. The New York Rangers invited him to their training camp at Winnipeg. Gordie was big for his age and plenty strong. But as a fifteen-year-old boy among grizzled NHL veterans he was awed, shy, and nervous. The veterans gave him a pretty bad time of it, and the combination of hazing, and homesickness, took its toll. He left camp.

A year later he was back, this time in the camp of the Detroit Red Wings where he promptly signed a contract and was assigned to a junior team. A Canadian amateur ruling prohibited him from playing that season, but two years later, in 1946, at the age of 18, he made the Red Wings and was there to stay.

Howe didn't make a big splash as a rookie—he scored just seven goals. But he began leaving his mark. On the team's first trip to Montreal he tangled with Rocket Richard and actually floored the Rocket with a punch. The angered Richard, instead of going after the youngster, slugged Howe's teammate, Sid Abel, who had made some remark.

The following year Gordie got 16 goals and the year after that, 1948–49, just 12. But that was the first year he was permanently united with center Sid Abel and left wing Ted Lindsay. Together, the trio formed the famous Production Line, and led the Wings through the most successful period in their history.

In the playoffs during that 1948–49 season, Gordie led his club with eight goals and 11 points. The following year he took off, ramming home 35 goals and picking up 33 assists for 68 points. He was on the brink of stardom when he suffered a severe, and almost permanent setback.

It was in the 1950 playoffs with Toronto, the third period of the opening game. Gordie was backchecking the Leafs' Ted Kennedy when he went hurtling into the boards, head first. He was rushed to the hospital. The diagnosis was a severe concussion with extreme pressure on the brain. A surgeon was brought in and an emergency operation performed. Without the operation, Howe surely would have died that night. As it was, he was close to death for several more days. Then, slowly, he began to recover.

Some thought he'd never play again, but when the next season started, there he was, raring to go. Gordie said he didn't remember what happened in that game with Toronto. Some said Kennedy caused the accident, others said it just happened. But the Gordie Howe who returned to the ice for the 1950–51 season was the Gordie Howe people would see for the next two decades, an uncompromisingly rugged player.

The season before, Howe's linemate Ted Lindsay, had taken the NHL scoring crown with 78 points. Howe came back to score 43 goals and 43 assists for 86 points and the first of four scoring titles in succession. As for the head injury, its only after-effect was a rapid, constant blinking of the eyes, something that certainly didn't hamper Gordie as a player or as an individual.

Throughout the early '50's, the Production Line continued as one of the most potent units in the NHL. And from 1948–49 to 1954–55, the Wings finished first during the regular season seven consecutive times, winning the post-season Stanley Cup four times. The season before and the season after that streak, the club was second, and they finished first again in 1956–57 for perhaps the most successful decade a team has ever had in league history.

During that decade, Gordie was making his mark as a great scorer. He had 47 goals in 1951–52, and 49 the next year. When he took another scoring title in 1956–57, he did it with 44 goals and 45 assists, and when he won his last point crown in 1962–63, he had 38 goals and 48 assists.

And in the 1968–69 season, playing full tilt at the age of 41, the amazing Gordie scored 44 goals and accumulated 59 assists for 103 points. He didn't lead the league that year (point totals after expansion were higher than ever), but it was a personal high and his assist mark set a record for right wingers. And the most amazing part was that he did this at an age when most players would have been relaxing in retirement.

Very few players took liberties with Gordie Howe. After his severe head injury, he rarely left himself open to rough stuff. In fact, he was often the aggressor doling out punishment before taking it himself. Even when he was pushing 40, very few younger players crossed his path with intent to do him harm. They knew.

It didn't really matter who the man was, if he pushed Gordie Howe too hard, he could expect the worst. The Rangers had a defenseman in the mid-'50's named Lou Fontinato, who became the scourge of the NHL. Fontinato was a hitter, a checker, a brawler, a fighter, and proud of it. In a short time he garnered a reputation as a man to be feared, one who could damage an entire opposing team singlehanded.

Fontinato meted out his personal brand of mayhem without prejudice. He hit everyone and anyone, including Gordie Howe. With Howe, he proceeded slowly, testing the veteran and finding out what he could get away with. Each time the Rangers met the Wings, Fontinato picked his spot and went after Howe. Detroit fans watched with surprise and bewilderment as their hero seemed to be taking Fontinato's best shots and not doing anything about it.

Then one night the two teams met in the Garden. Fontinato was feeling pretty frisky in front of his home fans and he began to work Howe over as the Ranger crowd roared its approval. Then the two went at it in the corner, Fontinato pushing, elbowing, gouging. The puck squirted out and they started up ice, Gordie skating behind tough Looie.

Suddenly, Fontinato was clutching at his ear, the blood gushing out of a severe cut. Howe was skating away, the picture of innocence. Fontinato had the necessary repairs and resumed playing in the next game without altering his style. And he still hadn't had his fill of Gordie Howe.

The next time the two teams met in the Garden, Looie wanted revenge. He waited for his chance. It came when Howe got into a stick-fencing duel with Eddie Shack. Fontinato was some 60 feet away when it started but he skated over to the fray and without a moment's hesitation began throwing punches at Howe. Shack stepped away to let the two go at it.

Gordie calmly dropped his gloves and went to work.

He set Fontinato up with short, crisp left jabs. Then he peppered the defenseman's face with sharp rights. Not even the ref risked getting in the way of Howe's flying fists. In a matter of seconds Fontinato's face was a bloody pulp. His nose was broken and sitting at almost a right angle from its original position. The officials and other players finally pulled Howe away, afraid of what he might do if he continued.

It was one of the most one-sided fights in the NHL. In fact, it received a full picture spread in a national magazine and the entire incident served to lessen Fontinato's effectiveness as a tough guy. And it established once and for all the reputation of Gordie Howe. Never again would anyone test Howe's mettle.

In the later years, some of Howe's opponents, themselves great hockey players, began to acknowledge the veteran star's abilities.

Goalie Gleen Hall, one of the best netminders of the modern era once said, "For my sake I hope Howe quits the game tomorrow. The man can beat you at any time from any angle and on any kind of shot."

Jean Beliveau, the great Canadien center called Howe "the best hockey player I've ever seen," while Bobby Hull, the famed "Golden Jet," lamented, "I'd just like to be half as good as Gordie." It's also been said that even the proud Rocket Richard has admitted that Howe was a better all-around player than he was.

There was little doubt of Gordie's overall abilities. During his middle years he was on the ice for almost 40 minutes a game, something not done since the old days. Not only did he take his regular line turn, but he killed penalties, worked on the power play, and occasionally played defense when the Wings had a deficiency on their backline. Those who knew him best said he could even have played goal if he wished. That's how good he was.

During Gordie's 20th season in the league when he was a ripe old 37-year-old, someone began clocking the various hockey players to see who was the fastest skater in the NHL. The great Bobby Hull came out on top, hitting a speed of 29.2 miles per hour. Frank Mahovlich was close behind at 29.1 mph, with Henri Richard, the Pocket Rocket, next at 28.9. To the surprise of many, old man Howe was close behind Richard, skating at a speed of 28.7 miles per hour.

But that's the beauty of Gordie Howe. He did things so effortlessly on the NHL ice that most people didn't even realize he could move that way. In his last years with the Wings, when he was conscious of pacing himself, he looked even more casual out there. Yet all the old skills were marvelously intact, and Gordie retained his effectiveness. It was a painful wrist injury, not old age, that forced his retirement. Now, at the age of 45, the grand old man of hockey is preparing for a comeback, to play alongside his sons in the WHA. But no matter how the experiment works out, nothing can tarnish the records Gordie Howe has compiled. Nothing can alter the fact that this man was undoubtedly the greatest all-around player in NFL history.

There have been many great players in the National Hockey League, a good number of them coming on since World War II. Rocket Richard and Gordie Howe, of course, are probably the two best known, but there is another player, another Montreal Canadien, who must be rated as one of the very best of all time.

His name is Jean Arthur Beliveau, Le Grand Beliveau, who played his way out of Rocket Richard's shadow to dominate Montreal hockey in the decade of the '60's. Beliveau was a center, a handsome French Canadian following the tradition of Howie Morenz and Elmer Lach, Les Canadiens' great centers of past years.

Yet Beliveau, as great a player as he was, brought something else as well to Montreal—a quality of elegance, of class, that has rarely been seen in the rough and tumble sport. Beliveau was a gentleman from the word go, a big, 6′ 3″, 205-pounder who disdained the brawling, fighting style of so many other big men.

That didn't detract from his skills. In the 18 seasons in which Beliveau performed for the Canadiens he scored 507 goals and picked up 712 assists for a total of 1,219 points, a figure which was second best to Gordie Howe's when Jean retired. Alex Delvecchio of Detroit has since moved into second place. Still, Beliveau is the highest-scoring center of all time, a multi-year all-star and captain of some of the greatest Canadien teams ever.

Beliveau went out on top. He retired at the end of the 1970–71 season after leading Les Canadiens to another Stanley Cup triumph. During that final season, the 39-year-old Beliveau played in 70 games, scored 25 goals and 51 assists for 76 points, and was even better than that in the playoffs. In 20 Stanley Cup games he got six goals and a record-setting 16 assists, still playing the game with his own particular kind of style and grace.

Yet there was a inner turmoil which almost destroyed the exterior calm of Beliveau and at one time came close to forcing a premature retirement. It was the pressure of being the Big Man, the center for the Montreal Canadiens. Jean had a tradition to follow and he often thought he wasn't living up to the legends. The fans in Montreal didn't help the situation, either.

They were used to the flamboyance of a Morenz or a Richard, and Beliveau's easy style didn't always suit them.

"There were times when it seemed as if I could never please the fans," Beliveau admitted. "If I'd get three goals in a game they'd want four or five . . . always more. One year I had 84 points, finishing third in scoring just five points from the leader. That wasn't good enough for them, either.

"Sometimes fans' reactions made me feel nauseous, physically sick. It reached a point where all I wanted to do was go straight home after a game and stay there until it was time for the next game. I was worried about my health and thought about retiring."

This was in the early 1960's, after Richard had left the game and the fans at the Forum were looking for another Rocket. But when Beliveau finally quit a decade later, they loved him as much as any of their former heroes, for they finally came to appreciate the way in which the big man played the game.

And he lent his own brand of modesty to areas outside the rink. Once, he was invited to represent his sport at a banquet in Rochester, New York, where Mickey Mantle was being presented the Hickock Belt as Athlete of the Year. Many crippled children from nearby hospitals were invited to see their favorite heroes.

There were superstars present from every sport, and each one got up to say a few words. Yet it was Jean Beliveau who drew the only standing ovation when he quietly finished his talk with the following words:

"Instead of us being honored, we athletes should thank God for being so kind of us. The real heroes are the children sitting here in front of us." Jean never had a good command of the English language, yet he said what was in his heart and said it well.

On the ice, Beliveau showed unconcern for the head-hunting tactics of other players. During a brawl with the Rangers, Believeau was acting as peacemaker when attacked by a lowly New York second-stringer. Asked by reporters if he'd be looking for the man next time, Beliveau replied:

"I'll be looking for two things, a win and the two points in the standings that go with it. Let's face it, there are some guys who don't really know how to play this game. So they act like woodchoppers and it keeps them in the league. So you can't really blame them for their actions."

It took a long time, but Beliveau's style finally won him admiration and respect. Conn Smythe, the founder of the Toronto Maple Leafs, said that "Jean Beliveau is the best thing ever to happen to modern hockey." And other people agreed. The big guy was truly someone special.

Jean Beliveau was born on August 31, 1931, in Three Rivers, Quebec. However, he grew up in nearby Victoriaville where he learned his hockey at the usual early age. Young Jean remained in Victoriaville, playing as much as he could and quickly becoming one of the best young players in the area. When the Victoriaville team folded, Beliveau moved on to Quebec City and that was when the pressure of the game first got to him.

As a junior, they said he'd be the best player in all Canada, and pretty soon he was. Then they said the same thing when he became a senior amateur player, and sure enough, Jean was quickly the best player in the country in his division. And his press clippings were beginning to precede his talents. Wherever he went, people expected to see a super player. When he wasn't extraordinary on a given night, they went home disappointed.

While still playing as an amateur with the Quebec Aces, Beliveau had two trial runs with the Canadiens. He played two games in 1950–51, and three more in the 1952–53 season. In those five contests he scored six goals and had an assist. Canadien fans wondered when Beliveau would be theirs full time. As for Jean, he was sorry about all the advance notice. He later said:

"I would have been better off if I came up a nobody. With all the notice, I started my career under all kinds of pressure."

Jean finally came up to stay in the 1953–54 season. And although his style dictated calmness, he was a nervous wreck. Injuries limited him to just 44 games that year and he finished with a modest 13 goals and 21 assists. But the next season he began opening up, banging home 37 scores and picking up 36 assists for 73 points, just two behind the leader. And in his third season he racked up 47 goals and added 41 assists to lead the league with 88 points, winning the Hart Trophy as MVP.

Some great years followed for Beliveau, and it looked as if he was finally living up to expectations. Then came the early 1960's and suddenly the big center was no longer the potent hockey force he had been. His point totals dropped. He went for long periods without scoring a goal. And he fretted about it.

"I used to have nightmares where I'd see goalies and open nets and all kinds of scoring chances, yet I couldn't deliver," he said. "During games I'd want to score so badly that I'd flub even the easy chances. It got so that I thought I'd never score again."

Beliveau had just 18 goals in 1961–62, and 18 more the next year. Two years after that he got just 20 and the fans were really on him. He was set to retire until the Canadien management talked him out of it. He finally rebounded with a 29-goal, 48-assist season in 1965–66. It had been a long road back.

Jean had been captain of the Canadiens since 1961, but he always wondered if he deserved that honor. More pressure. It wasn't until the mid-60's that he started to feel he was doing the job.

"For the first time Beliveau knows the players are looking to him as their leader," wrote one reporter. "Most of the other veterans from the '50's are gone and this has helped his confidence. He doesn't have any more doubts about his role."

So the big guy continued to play great hockey, right up until that final season of 1970–71. And those lucky enough to watch the final game of the Stanley Cup championships that year, witnessed the moving sight of Jean Beliveau skating around the Montreal Forum, holding the ancient silver trophy high above his head to the accompanying roar of his adoring fans. It was a moment Le Grand Beliveau will never forget.

When Eddie Shore retired from hockey in 1940, the guessing-game started as to who would be the game's next great defenseman. Strangely enough, when the man finally came along some seven years later, he was as much like Eddie Shore as a hummingbird is like a gorilla.

Doug Harvey played hockey in an easy, almost lazy kind of way. His face was expressionless, his movements, though purposeful, were deliberate. He rarely lost his cool, didn't fight and brawl, and didn't send opposing players to the hospitals with gashes and broken bones. He simply played hockey, using an intelligent flawless approach, and exerting a quiet, but steady leadership from the backline that made him one of the game's best players.

Harvey spent his glory years with the Montreal Canadiens, winning the James Norris Memorial Trophy as the league's best defenseman some seven times, and making the league's first all-star team on ten occasions. On the ice, he did everything well.

Off the ice, Harvey might be considered something of a flake. He enjoyed the game and liked a good time. He won the Norris Trophy for the sixth time in 1961, but when that season ended, the Canadiens for some reason thought their 36-year-old star was slowing down. So they shipped him to the Rangers for another defenseman, rugged Lou Fontinato.

When he arrived in New York, Harvey found himself named playing-coach of the team. All he did that year was lead the Rangers to a playoff berth for the first time in several seasons and win himself another Norris Trophy. His backline play was as good as ever. Just when it seemed that Doug had secured a nice niche for himself at New York, he announced he was giving up his coaching duties. Why?

"Aw, what the heck," he said in a slow drawl. "When I was coaching I couldn't be one of the boys. Now, if I want a beer with them, I can get a beer."

It was as if his slow, easy style on the ice carried over to his personal life. He wanted no part of the big-pressure situation involved in coaching. When Harvey finally dropped out of the NHL several years later he didn't leave the game and seek out a new career. The best defenseman in two decades continued to play hockey *in the minor leagues!*

Humiliating? Not to Harvey. He didn't care. He

was just doing his thing and having fun. Pretty soon he was coaching again, this time the Kansas City team in the Central Pro League. And, of course, he was the team's best defenseman.

By the 1967-68 season, the NHL had expanded and the Kansas City team was affiliated with the new St. Louis Blues of the NHL's Western Division. When the Blues needed a defenseman at the tail end of the season and for the playoffs, Coach Scotty Bowman persuaded Harvey to join the team. So there he was again, a 43-year-old veteran, still playing it slow and easy, and still making all the right plays, all the right passes, and the right stops.

He played one more full year for St. Louis, helping the younger players and helping the team. Then, he finally quit.

"Ive never met a player who puts my heart in my mouth as often as Doug," said his long-time coach at Montreal, Toe Blake. "His style is casual, but somehow it works and I've learned to swallow in silence. He makes a minimum number of mistakes and almost always anticipates the pass correctly. Yet I always said that he plays defense in a rocking chair."

Sometimes it seemed that Doug played with a trace of a smile on his cherubic face, even when he was involved in those head-on collisions that occur so often on the ice. Nothing bothered him.

One writer called Harvey's style a "flaw": "He was so laconic in style, so calmly sure of himself, that he executed plays of extreme complication with ease. Harvey lacked the flamboyance of Eddie Shore or some of the other Hall of Fame backliners, and because of this he was slow to receive the acclaim he deserved."

Another writer was equally impressed with Harvey's coolness. "His cool was often mistaken for disinterest," the man wrote. "But, actually, it was the result of an always calculating concentration."

Once in a game against the New York Rangers, Harvey slammed into the Rangers' Red Sullivan and sent the Blueshirt to the hospital with a ruptured spleen. It was a severe injury and Harvey was accused of having done it intentionally. It's extremely doubtful that Doug wanted to rupture Sullivan's spleen, but he did intend to show the New Yorker he meant business.

Harvey said that Sullivan had a habit of kicking opponents' skates, a dangerous maneuver that could result in a bad fall and head injury. Harvey claimed he warned Sullivan about this several times with no results. From there it was back to the basic rule of the jungle—survival.

So there were times when Doug showed emotion. His cool was saved for clutch game situations and that was why Rocket Richard felt he was so great. No matter how hot and heavy the action, the Rocket would say, Doug stays calm. In that sense, the Rocket felt Harvey had the perfect attitude.

After the glory years, Harvey was often criticized for continuing to play hockey. It was as if the purists didn't want to see the master's reputation tarnished. But Doug was doing what he wanted to do. What's more, he once said, "The money's not the best in the American League (the minor league), but it's not the worst either."

That was the Doug Harvey saga. He was a great defenseman in his time, not really like the Bobby Orrs or Brad Parks of today because he wasn't nearly as offense-minded as they were, although he was known as a fine rusher and puck carrier. Yet when the book closed it was Montreal coach Toe Blake who put the final words to the Doug Harvey story. Said Blake:

"Doug Harvey was the greatest defenseman who ever played hockey—bar none. Most defensemen specialize in one thing and build their reputations on that. Doug was unique. He could do everything well."

Hockey goaltending is one of the toughest, most physically wearing, most nerve-shattering positions in all of sports. Throughout NHL history there are stories of goaltenders succumbing to frayed nerves.

Bill Durnan, a six-time Vezina Trophy winner with the Canadiens, walked out during the Stanley Cup playoffs, his nerves shot. Glenn Hall, one of the best and coolest in the nets, often vomited before games. Roger Crozier needed major stomach surgery to correct a condition that was probably caused by nerves.

Yet some goalies go on and on, playing well into their 40's. Jacques Plante was out of hockey three years when he suddenly returned to the wars. Hall threatened to quit almost every year after he was 30. Crozier returned to the nets with half a stomach.

They returned to a job that has them guarding a four-foot-high, six-foot-wide cage against a small, hard rubber disk, which can be fired at them at 125 miles per hour or more. Even with pads, protection, and masks, it's a dangerous business.

In the old days, each team had only one goalie. The man played every minute of every game, no matter what. In cases of dire emergency, a house goalie was sometimes available. He was a man who came to the games and could suit up for either team. But, often, he wasn't a professional, and he was very rarely used. Goalies were tough guys. They just didn't quit.

When the schedule grew and the league expanded, the job became too demanding for one man. It's nearly impossible for one goalie to play 70-78 games a year.

So the two-goalie system has evolved, with teams dressing a pair of netminders, ideally of equal or nearly equal ability. These men split the schedule, with perhaps the better of the two playing a bit more and appearing in most of the big games against the better teams.

There have been many great goaltenders in postwar hockey. Their names click off the tongues of knowledgeable fans: Frankie Brimsek, Mr. Zero of the Boston Bruins; a pair of great Montrealers, Bill Durnan and Jacques Plante; Turk Broda of Toronto; Chuck Rayner of New York; Harry Lumley of Toronto; Glenn Hall, who played and starred with three clubs; and Johnny Bower, who still played like a kid at 45.

But one man in particular epitomized all the good and bad in NHL goaltending; Terry Sawchuk.

Sawchuk toiled for five different clubs during his National Hockey League career. He played for some 20 seasons and hung up 105 regular-season shutouts, the best total of any goalie in history.

What made this man a goalie and what kept him in the nets despite the bad luck that dogged his career?

Sawchuk was born on December 28, 1929, in the East Kildonan section of Winnipeg, Manitoba. He was a tough little kid they called "Butch," and would often mix it up with the other neighborhood youths. When he was just 10, he got his first goalkeeping equipment, but it came to him through tragedy. An older brother, who was already playing goal for a local team, died suddenly of a heart ailment and the Sawchuks gave his gear to young Terry.

Two years later, Terry ran into some trouble of his own. He was injured in a baseball game with the result that his right arm was shortened by two inches and the elbow joint was permanently stiffened, so he couldn't touch his right shoulder with his right hand.

Yet as soon as the injury healed, Terry was back in the nets. An NHL career became a goal early in his life and an obsession later. Old friends recall that Terry wouldn't even attend a movie as a youngster for fear that the glare would hurt his eyes. Later, he extended the ban to include textbooks.

Whether or not Terry's eye-saving activities helped is a matter of conjecture. But there's no disputing that young Sawchuk had phenomenal success at an early age. He joined the United States League at the age of 18 and was promptly named Rookie of the Year. The next season he was already a pro in the American League and was voted again the top rookie in the loop. Two years later, during the 1949–50 season, Terry donned the uniform of the Detroit Red Wings and at the season's end was—you guessed it—Rookie of the Year in the National Hockey League.

A year later Sawchuk was a first-team NHL all-star, and the year after that, again a first-team star, he put on a performance in the Stanley Cup playoffs that will never be forgotten. Playing in eight consecutive games, Sawchuk and the Wings swept the playoffs with the goalie producing four shutouts and allowing just five goals in the other four games. His goals-against average was a microscopic 0.62 per game.

But bad luck was still dogging him. In 1948, before he joined the Wings, he had to have three stitches taken directly in his right eyeball as the result of a stick slash. That same year he suffered an appendectomy. His third pro season was shortened by severe chest injuries suffered in a car accident. Eye trouble led to rumors of retirement in 1954.

All this caused the Wings to trade him to the Bruins in 1955, a strain that Terry couldn't take. He played, but not as well, and quit the team midway through the

1957 season. His nerves were on edge, he came down with a case of mononucleosis . . . he was a wreck.

Nevertheless, Detroit took a chance on him again in 1957, though his weight was down from 215 to 165. He was examined by a doctor and found to be on the edge of an emotional breakdown. When Terry was healthy and right there was none better, but troubles seemed to follow him. He went to Toronto in 1964 and two years later had to undergo a delicate spinal fusion operation. Yet he returned to the nets and starred in the Stanley Cup playoffs of 1967.

The next year he was with the expansionist L.A. Kings, then it was back to Detroit, and finally on to New York where he backed up Ed Giacomin. There, it ended for Terry. Lady Luck deserted him for good. Engaged in horseplay with a teammate, Sawchuk took a bad fall. He sustained severe internal injuries, and for the first time, Terry couldn't lick it. He died in a New York hospital in 1970.

Why do so many people call Terry Sawchuk the greatest netminder ever despite his career of ups and downs? There have been bouncier, quicker goalies, and goalies with better reflexes. Sawchuk's forte was studying the game and its shooters and knowing what a given forward could do with the puck at a given angle.

And Sawchuk was number one at playing angles, that is, leaving exposed only the toughest part of the net for a forward to shoot at from a given position on the ice. If a player is coming down the ice on the right side of the goalie, the goalie moves to his right, protecting that side of the cage and forcing the shooter to try for a tiny opening on his near side or a difficult angle shot at the bigger opening on the far side.

Sawchuk was a marvel at moving back and forth in

his crease, sometimes just an inch or two, in order to make it more difficult to score. It's said that Terry took more shots head-on than any other goalie. People in the stands might say "easy save" when they saw it happen, but they didn't realize that Sawchuk had set it up.

Another trump card was Terry's sense of anticipation. By always knowing exactly where he was relative to the cage behind him, he had a good idea where the shooter would try to put the puck and he was ready to make the save in that spot. Sometimes he would intentionally leave an area of the goal exposed, inviting the forward to shoot at it. But he'd be ready and make the save look easy.

Last but not least, Terry had the indomitable spirit that characterizes the great goalie. Perhaps this story best illustrates it: Sawchuk was playing for the Leafs against the Chicago Black Hawks. As usual, he was bruised and battered from the previous weeks' play. Bobby Hull, the Golden Jet, had the puck some 15 feet to Sawchuk's left. His stick flashed and he unleashed that booming slapshot. The puck struck Terry's left shoulder and he went down as if he'd been shot.

The Maple Leaf trainer rushed out and got to the goalie just as Terry was getting to his knees.

"Where'd you get hit?" he asked.

"On my bad shoulder," said Sawchuk, painfully.

"Do you think you'll be all right?"

At that, Sawchuk stood up, picked up his gloves and stick and started smoothing the ice in the goal crease. Then he looked up angrily at the trainer and the players around him.

"I stopped the damned shot, didn't I?" said Terry Sawchuk.

4   *The Expansion Drama*

IF YOU HAD told someone a few years earlier that a major sport was going to double in size in just one year you would have heard the laughter, loud and long. Yet in 1967 the NHL did just that.

Of course the league had added teams before. During the first part of the century when things were still taking shape, franchises came and went like feathers in the wind, and the league grew slowly.

There was a time of mild expansion in the '20's when U.S. teams joined the NHL. Then after the years of attrition in the '30's came another rise in popularity and financial prosperity.

By the '50's Minor League hockey was moving south and west, and finding acceptance among new groups of fans. By 1956, NHL hockey was beginning to appear on television screens, giving the game even more exposure, and soon the writers and broadcasters began harping on the need for new teams.

"The National Hockey League makes a mockery of its title by restricting its franchises to six teams, waging a kind of private little tournament of 70 games just to eliminate two teams," said one writer, talking about the four-team Stanley Cup system.

Another pointed out that other major sports were expanding and that hockey couldn't sit there forever, standing pat on an old formula. Still another pictured the NHL as "a tight little island of closefisted, inbred standpatters with a stranglehold on a grand professional game."

By the early 1960's fans were jamming the turnstyles in all cities of the six NHL franchises. Often they were turned away in droves. In Montreal, a season ticket was the most prized possession a person could have, and many were known to have their ducats on the top of the list when their wills were read.

Other cities faced an increase in "scalpers," who managed to get tickets and would sell them outside the stadiums for large profit. All the scalper had to do was stand there, because there were hundreds of people walking around asking if anyone had tickets to sell. With demand at an all-time level, expansion made good sense.

If the NHL didn't do it, someone else would. Sure enough, there were rumblings about a new professional league springing up in western Canada and the west coast of the United States. A talent war would cause more trouble and cost more money than it was worth. It was time to act.

How to expand was another problem. At that time, four of the six teams qualified for the Stanley Cup, still the greatest prize in hockey. If new teams were added to the present division, it would just mean more non-qualifiers. Hockey may have learned a lesson from baseball. In that sport, new teams with no chance of a pennant quickly lost any initial followings they might have gathered.

There was an alternative, and the league's expansion committee, led by David Molson of the Canadiens and William Jennings of the Rangers, liked it very much. They would create an entire new division, six teams, which would compete with the older established teams in limited interdivisional play. Four of the six new teams would also qualify for post-season playoff action, giving the fans some added excitement and offering them at least the possibility of a Stanley Cup championship.

This seemed to be the best way to do it. Next came the selection of the new teams. In March of 1965, NHL president Clarence Campbell made a short announcement:

"The National Hockey League proposes to expand its operations through the formation of a second six-team division. Applications will be accepted from responsible groups representing major league cities in the United States and Canada, and when six new teams are accepted the new division will be incorporated into the league.

"The six cities which will make up the new division must be of major league status and have arenas with permanent seating capacities and ice surfaces meeting current NHL standards. The new franchise owners must either own the arena or have long-term leases thereof.

"The new division will play a partially interlocking schedule with the present six teams of the NHL. Sufficient players will be made available by the present teams for purchase by the new division."

That was it, and the scramble was on. It was to cost a new franchise only two million dollars to get in the league—a low price. Selecting the new sites wasn't easy. Politics and infighting began quickly.

It went without saying that the West Coast would get two franchises. That would make hockey stretch from coast to coast and would also end any threat of a rival league in that region. The rest were up for grabs. Some logical cities were denied. Toronto opposed Buffalo because the two cities were just 100 miles apart. The two Canadian teams were against a Vancouver franchise because of TV monopolies in all of Canada. So that western Canadian city lost out.

When the final decision was made, the new teams would be based in Los Angeles, Oakland (with drawing power in San Francisco), St. Louis, Minneapolis-St. Paul, Philadelphia, and Pittsburgh. Canadians were outraged by the decision. Their national game was being taken from them and they couldn't understand why. Perhaps they should have asked the two incumbent Canadian teams and they would have found out.

At any rate, the details were quickly worked out so the new teams could begin play in the 1967–68 season. The schedule was increased from 70 to 74 games. Each team would play 50 games within its division (meeting each opponent ten times) and 24 games against the other division (four games with each team). That way, they reasoned, imbalance between old and new teams could be held to a minimum.

There was also a plan for supplying players. The old teams could protect one goalie and 11 other players from their rosters of 18 men. When the new teams picked a player, the old team could freeze another. In other words, each old team would lose its 12th, 14th, 16th, and 18th players. Then the new teams would get a shot at minor leaguers and free agents.

Some people figured the new teams weren't getting

much. They could get a quality netminder if they were lucky, but after that they'd have just a handful of proven players. But expansion was good for some old-timers, who got a chance to come out of the minors for one final fling. Many produced some good hockey.

One quality player who thought expansion worked well was Ed Van Impe, a defenseman picked from Chicago by Philadelphia. Said Van Impe: "The whole thing (expansion) was good for hockey. The new teams were good teams. Let's face it, a lot of good hockey players never really had a chance until now. When you start with 120 open spots and suddenly increase it to 240, a lot of players will get new life. And a lot of them will prove they belong."

The first year of expansion play surprised everyone. Not only did the Western Division play good hockey, but the six clubs took a surprising 33 percent of their possible points against Eastern teams. St. Louis actually won the Western playoffs that year although they lost the Cup to Montreal in four straight.

In 1968–69 one change was made. Attendance at Pittsburgh, Los Angeles, and Oakland wasn't very good and the owners thought they had a solution. Bring in the Eastern teams more often and let the fans get more looks at Bobby Hull, Gordie Howe, Bobby Orr, and the other great players. The teams would play 40 games in their own division and 36 in the other, for a total of 76 games.

All the problems of expansion were not solved, however. The Western teams suddenly began floundering against Eastern opponents, taking only about 30 percent of the possible points. Some hockey observers thought they had the answer. In the first year of expansion, the Western teams were stocked with many veterans and rejects who wanted desperately to prove themselves against the Eastern teams. These men were skyhigh for interdivisional games and played over their heads. Now things were evening out. In the Cup final, Montreal once again whipped the St. Louis Blues, four games to none.

In the third season, panic set in. The Western teams got just 28 percent of the possible points against the East. And in the Cup final, the Boston Bruins buried the St. Louis Blues in four straight. In effect, the Eastern Division final was actually determining the Stanley Cup winner. The playoff series with the West was becoming a joke.

As a result, in the 1970–71 season more changes were made. New franchises appeared in Buffalo and Vancouver (Canada finally got one), and they were added to the Eastern Division. The Chicago Black Hawks, who had won the East the previous year, moved over to the West. With a 14-team league, the schedule was upped to 78 games and each club played the other six times, regardless of division.

Now it was the fans' turn to moan. Traditional opponents only played each other a half dozen times, meaning local fans could see heated rivalries, such as the Rangers and Bruins, only three times a season. Playoff procedure was also changed, with a cross-over system in the second round, meaning that two Eastern teams or two Western teams could meet in the Cup final. This made it more likely for the two best teams to face each other in the last round.

There was another byproduct of expansion: Scoring totals soared. Before expansion, Bobby Hull had held the record for points in a season with 97. The first year of expansion, his teammate Stan Mikita tied it. Then, in 1968–69, with more games being played against the Western Division, things changed.

Boston center Phil Esposito checked in with 49 goals and 77 assists for a whopping 126 points. The same year the remarkable Gordie Howe, at the age of 41, had 103 points. The next season, defenseman Bobby Orr led the league with 120 points on 33 goals and 87 assists. And in 1970–71, with expansion to 14 teams, Esposito wound up with 76 goals and 76 assists for 152 points, breaking all marks. Orr was second that year, garnering 102 assists during the course of the campaign.

There was a time when the 20-goal scorer in the NHL was equated with a .300 hitter in baseball. Now, the 30-goal scorer has that distinction, and the 20-goal man is probably down around .275.

In spite of growing pains, expansion has worked well for the sport. The New York Islanders and Atlanta Flames joined the league in 1972–73, making the NHL a 16-team league with the prospect of more to come. Attendance in most new cities continues to be good and the old cities continue to be sold out. The new draft system, which was inaugurated in 1967, promises to give the poor teams first chance at the outstanding amateurs. Buffalo is a perfect example of an expansionist team building through the draft. One year the Sabres picked up Gilbert Perreault, and the next Rick Martin. Both were instant superstars and gave the Sabres a major league attack.

So everything seemed to be working smoothly for the National Hockey League. There was talk of a four-division league someday, and even some dreamy conjecture about teams in Europe and in Russia competing in the NHL in the future. But then, in 1971, a big monkey wrench was tossed into the hopper.

It was called the World Hockey Association. It began in the summer of '71 when a group of business-

men met in New York and announced that the new
league, a rival professional league, would begin play at
the outset of the 1972–73 season. Most hockey people
met the news with belly laughs. How could a league
be organized and ready to start so soon?

But the WHA people weren't fooling. They began
ticking off a list of cities that would be given franchises.
NHL president Clarence Campbell gave the old
league's first reaction to the insurgents.

"We all wish them well," said the wily Campbell.
"To tell the truth I'm pleased that hockey has become
so successful that more people want to get into the
business. But I hope they don't start to steal our players, because if they do that we'll fight them from the
ramparts."

Stealing players was what new leagues were all about.
It happened with the American Football League before
the merger and was happening with the American Basketball Association. There was no reason to believe it
wouldn't happen if a new hockey league came into being.

The NHL moved into action. They hastened their
expansion, bringing New York Islanders and Atlanta
Flames into the league two years earlier than planned.
This shut off the Nassau Coliseum and Atlanta's new
arena as possible WHA sites. It finally took a court
order to get the WHA the use of Madison Square Garden for its New York franchise and the team had to
take the second choice in dates and game times.

But the WHA was working fast, too. The league
tapped the vast Canadian market by setting up franchises in Alberta, Ottawa, Quebec, and Winnipeg.
There were also teams going into Cleveland and Houston. And the new league went head-on against the NHL
in Chicago, Los Angeles, Minnesota, New England

(Boston based), New York, and Philadelphia. It was certainly an ambitious undertaking. The bettors were saying it wouldn't happen.

But before long it was obvious that the new league was working. Second-line and marginal NHL players began to jump over, simply because the WHA was offering more money than they might ever make in the NHL. The new league also went after Canada's vast resources of amateurs. Even though the NHL helped the amateur leagues survive, the players could sign wherever they chose. In addition, the WHA grabbed players still in their teens, ignoring the 20-year-old rule imposed by the NHL. So, in that respect, they were beating the NHL to the punch.

Still, it looked doubtful. Then in the summer of 1972, the league pulled a coup. A new conference was called in Winnipeg where it was announced that Bobby Hull, the great star of the Chicago Black Hawks, was joining the Winnipeg Jets of the WHA as player-coach on a 10-year deal worth upwards of two million dollars.

Suddenly, the WHA was *real!* Bobby Hull was perhaps hockey's most dynamic player of the past decade, a man who went over the 50-goal mark five times. That started it. The big money came out and the offers began to roll.

Derek Sanderson, the popular, charismatic center of the Boston Bruins, jumped to the Philadelphia Blazers for a reported $2.75 million. His coach would be Johnny McKenzie, another long-time Bruin favorite.

Two top goalies were the next to go over: Bernie Parent of Toronto and Gerry Cheevers of Boston. All-star defenseman J. C. Trembley of the Canadiens accepted a player-coach deal from the Quebec Nordiques. Jim Dorey of New York and Ted Green of Boston signed with the New England Whalers. Other players followed, not superstars, but good players, enough to give the WHA some identity and some representative hockey.

The NHL smarted at the loss of talent, but they were powerless to do anything about it. Some teams took their cases to court in order to prevent jumping players from competing, but that was merely a temporary holding tactic. The best way to prevent jumps was to renegotiate contracts. The Rangers were one team that did this to a high degree.

New York knew that the WHA was making offers to its big stars, men like Brad Park, Walt Tkaczuk, and the GAG Line of Vic Hadfield, Jean Ratelle, and Rod Gilbert. All received generous, multiyear contracts to remain Rangers.

As the WHA got off the ground, attendance in many cities was poor. Only a star like Hull could pack them in. The brand of hockey was good, though certainly inferior to the NHL. Only the top teams, New England (which won the WHA's World Cup), Winnipeg, and perhaps Cleveland could compete on an NHL level. Scores were high and play loose. But the league had some attractive innovations, such as overtime periods to avert tie games, and it made it through the first season.

There was some trouble with the big stars. Hull was kept out of action for awhile by the courts, but still ended up with 50 goals and was MVP. Sanderson never played much, was injured, finally settled his contract and went back to the Bruins. Parent quit the Blazers at the outset of the playoffs.

But mishaps always occur in a new league, no matter what the sport. When players get enormous contracts, with all kinds of fine print, there's bound to be bad blood and court action sooner or later. But the league-jumping continues, with more NHL players taking big-money offers and bolting.

Whether the WHA will survive or not is still a question mark. For all intents and purposes it got off to a good start. The new league hasn't hurt NHL attendance, though it's cost the owners more money in salaries and has taken some of the top stars away from their NHL teams. But what it's really done is add to the expansion of professional hockey. Less than 10 years ago there were six professional teams. Now there are some 28 franchises operating in the United States and Canada.

The quality of play has had to change. Suddenly, more than four times as many players are professionals, and all of them can't be as good as the small group that operated in the old NHL as recently as 1966. But the wide-open, often high-scoring style of today is perfectly suited to the increased television and media exposure. There are more "personalities" in hockey than ever before and the fans love a 35-goal scorer more than a 15-goal man. It's just something that happens, similar to football fans wanting to meet a 1,000-yard runner as opposed to a guy who gained just 400.

Hockey will continue go grow and expand, as long as the fans keep pouring through the gate and the demand for new franchises proliferates. The shape and form of the expansion are the only questions. Will the WHA make it? Will hockey go international? These are the questions that must be answered. And only time will tell.

5   *The Seventies' Superstars*

THERE HAVE BEEN many good hockey players down through the years. The number thins when you talk about very good hockey players, and becomes even smaller when you count superstars. The very special players don't come along too often, although many players put together super seasons every now and then, and sometimes even run two or three of them together.

But when the books close, there are very few Vezinas, Morenzes, Shores, Richards, Harveys, Sawchuks, and Howes. The true superstars keep their standard of performance at top level, year after year after year.

What about today? How many of these very special players are currently performing in the professional ranks? After all, with almost four times as many teams in action there's a better chance to find the superstars.

Some of today's players have already earned the title of superstars, players such as Bobby Hull, Bobby Orr, Phil Esposito, and Stan Mikita, just to name four. Others are on the brink of superstardom—a Frank Mahovlich or Jean Ratelle, for example. Still others, young players, are rapidly coming into the pattern that could lead to superstardom. Gil Perreault has been called the new Beliveau. Bobby Clarke gets better each year and has already been voted MVP. And there are others.

What puts these men at the top of their profession?

BOBBY HULL

They call him the "Golden Jet," a nickname acquired in his early years when a bright mane of blond hair flowed freely in the breeze. The passing time has thinned the hair a bit, but the Jet is as fast as ever.

Robert Marvin Hull, the man who made the slapshot the most feared weapon in the game, never stops making hockey news. His first 604 goals came in the National Hockey League; his next 50 were earned in the World Hockey Association, as he became the first established superstar to jump over to the rival league.

They say Hull did it for money. He says so, too, and no one can fault him for that. Even if he jumped to the Disneyland Kiddie League (if there was one) it wouldn't dim his great hockey feats.

Six times in a 16-year career Bobby Hull has scored 50 or more goals in a season. In the mid-60's he was the NHL's fastest skater (a scientifically proven fact) and possessor of the league's hardest shot. There were those who said he was also the strongest player in the league. He not only skated a regular turn on left wing for the Chicago Black Hawks, but he killed penalties and worked the power play as well. He was often on the ice upwards of 40 minutes per game.

As a goal scorer, Hull holds some impressive records. For instance, Bobby holds the record for the most consecutive 30-goal seasons in succession. He had 13 of them, not counting his first year in the WHA. The closest mark to that is six, by Phil Esposito of the Bruins. Hull also has scored three or more goals in a game some 28 times in his NHL career, two better than an old timer named Cy Denneny and a not-so-old timer named Maurice Richard. He's also had eight 40-goal NHL seasons, with his closest rivals being Howe and Esposito with five each.

There's nothing that Bobby Hull can't do on a hockey rink. Some will say, however, that he's too nice out there—that if he had Howe's temperament he'd have been an even greater player. Because of Bobby's great speed and skating ability, rival players often resort to less than legal maneuvers in trying to stop him. He's been pushed, held, grabbed, tripped, gouged, elbowed . . . you name it.

Yet Bobby Hull has generally tried to fight back with his ability alone, by scoring goals. Rarely, especially in his first ten years, would he used Howe's tactics to let opponents know they'd better let up. In fact, Bobby has been a winner of the Lady Byng Trophy, an annual trophy given to the player best exhibiting a combination of ability and good sportsmanship.

But no matter what his opponents have tried, they haven't found a way to stop Bobby Hull. His slapshot has been clocked at almost 130 miles per hour, and with power like that, he's a threat to score from anywhere on the ice.

In fact, it was the disarming velocity of Hull's shot that led to the ban on overly curved sticks some years ago. One day in practice, Hull's teammate on the Black Hawks, Stan Mikita, broke the blade of his stick. Just for kicks he continued to play with it. The break had given the blade a strange shape, almost a curve, and

Mikita found that when he shot the puck with the stick, the rubber disk did strange things, breaking and dipping, must like a spitball in baseball.

He soon told Hull about the phenomenon, and the two superstars bent some sticks under a door frame and began using them in games. It was bad enough letting a slick player like Mikita use the new weapon, but in Hull's hands it was deadly. Goalies didn't know what to do about the dipping and curving bullets that the Golden Jet was firing at them. Soon, other players around the league were curving their sticks and goalies were running for the hills.

It wasn't long before league officials saw the potential danger in the overly curved sticks, and they limited the curve to just one-half inch. Mostly because of Hull.

Once Hull got up a full head of steam in the NHL, people began comparing him with other greats. Sid Abel, a long-time NHL player and coach, cited one basic difference between Hull and Richard: "I think Bobby works harder than the Rocket for his goals," Abel said, "because he carries the puck while the Rocket always had the puck given to him."

Stafford Smythe, president of the Toronto Maple Leafs had this to say after Bobby had been in the league about seven years: "Hull is the best and most colorful hockey player in the game. He has it all, great talent, a world of desire, and consistency. Plus he's getting stronger and better every season."

The word from the great Gordie Howe was quick and to the point. "Bobby skates so fast that when he's on the ice everybody else in the league feels slower."

The fact that Hull was a target not only for frustrated defensemen but young players, too, was pointed out by Bob Plager, who was at one time fighting to win a regular job on the St. Louis Blues' backline.

After running at Hull several times during the course of a game with the Black Hawks, Plager said:

"People notice it when you hit Hull."

Perhaps the best example of Hull as the complete hockey player can be drawn from a change that occurred between the 1968–69 and 1969–70 seasons. The Hawks were floundering a bit that first year—that is, all except Hull. He was scoring at a record pace. When the season ended, Bobby had set a new record (at that time) of 58 goals for the year. The team, however, finished dead last in the Eastern Division. That's when Coach Billy Reay had a talk with Bobby.

Reay knew that Hull felt he often had to do it all by himself on the ice. As a result, he'd become much too goal-oriented and was inadvertently letting up on his backchecking and defensive assignments. Reay was attempting to remold the entire club and asked Bobby to lead the way.

The next season Hull played differently. He passed more, concentrated on defense, and avoided his exciting one-man rushes at the net. Despite missing some 14 games, he still managed 38 goals. But more important, he led the new-style Hawks from the bottom to the top. They finished first, marking the only time in league history that a team has done such a complete turnabout in one year.

"I was less of an individual that year," remarked Hull. "I became more conscious of the five other guys out on the ice with me."

As with most Canadian players, hockey and Bobby Hull go a long way back together. Bobby was born in Point Anne, Ontario, on January 3, 1939. His father had wanted to be a hockey player, and he was determined that his first-born son should have his chance.

When Bobby was three, he got his first pair of skates, a Christmas present from his father.

There was a lake right across the street, and Bobby's two olders sisters took the three-year-old over to it. Within a few hours young Bobby was skating without support and he went at it all afternoon until dinner. He got his first stick the next year.

When Bobby was five years old, he remembers he'd get up at 5 A.M. and go out to skate. It was so cold that when he returned he'd have to warm his hands by the fire to get the circulation back. Mr. Hull recalls sneaking down to the lake to watch his son one morning: "I couldn't believe my eyes," he said. "Bobby was handling the stick and making plays as well as boys twice his age. I knew then that he'd be in the National Hockey League someday. I just knew it."

By the time Bobby was 12 he was holding his own against grown men. He was already his team's fastest skater and was on his way to acquiring his great strength. There seemed to be no stopping him.

At about that time Bob Wilson, a scout for the Chicago Black Hawks, spotted Bobby and put the youngster on the Hawks' negotiation list with the NHL. Under the rules then in force, Bobby's future was set. If he was going to play pro hockey, the Hawks had the first rights to sign him.

Bobby signed his letter of intent two years later, and was sent to a boarding school in Hespeler, Ontario, the real reason being to teach him a better brand of hockey. Bobby was extremely homesick at first, but slowly got used to his new routine.

The hours of practice paid off. Bobby was a star in the juniors for two years, then moved up to the Junior A League, and at the age of 18 was ready for the big time—his NHL debut.

In the fall of 1957, the 18-year-old Hull was still in high school at St. Catharines. He only played hockey on the weekends; during the week he was a fullback on the school's football team. One afternoon he had a big game, gaining good yardage against a tough defense and scoring two touchdowns. He got back to the boarding house, bruised and battered from the afternoon's play, and learned that Bob Wilson was calling him.

"Hurry down to the rink," Wilson snapped. "The Black Hawks want you to play in the exhibition game against the Rangers tonight."

Bobby bolted his dinner and left. That night, playing against NHL competition for the first time in his life, Bobby Hull blasted home two goals. He was in the league to stay.

Hull scored just 13 goals that year, losing out in the Rookie of the Year balloting to another left wing, Frank Mahovlich of Toronto. The next year Bobby collected 18 scores. Then, in the spring of 1959, he accompanied an NHL all-star team on a tour of Europe and there, he says, he learned to play hockey.

"I learned to pace myself when I went on that trip," Bobby recalls. "Up to that time I used to go all out, all the time, carrying the puck every chance I had and really working for every shot, every rush up ice. During the tour I played a lot on a line with Eddie Shack, and Eddie liked to carry the puck as much as I did. Suddenly I realized I didn't have to do all the work all the time. I was just as effective, even more effective sometimes, when he carried and I waited for the pass. I got 15 goals in 21 games and used the same style when I started the 1959–60 NHL season."

That year Bobby exploded for 39 goals and 42 assists, giving him 81 points and his first Art Ross Trophy as scoring champion. He was 21 and the second youngest player ever to win the point title. He got 31 the next season, but in 1961–62, he showed what was to come by blasting home 50 goals. He was only the third player in history to hit the magic mark.

He took a second scoring championship that year. With the Hawks' surprise Stanley Cup victory the season before, Bobby Hull had achieved quite a bit by the time he was 23 years old.

From there, it was just super play every year for Bobby. He had 39 goals and 32 assists in 1964–65, but his all-around play was so outstanding that he was named winner of the Hart Trophy as the league's MVP, and also took the Lady Byng for his conduct on the ice.

It was hard to believe that Bobby Hull could get any better, but he did. In the next four seasons he scored 54, 52, 44, and 58 goals, each figure leading the league, for an average of 52 a year.

There were injuries over the years, mostly minor, nagging ones, but like most NHL stars, Bobby played through them. Some of the hurts were caused by over-aggressive defensemen. Bobby accepted them as part of the game. Sometimes, it bothered other players more than it did Hull to see the way his rivals blatantly fouled him. After one game, Bobby's teammate Stan Mikita said:

"Bobby and I have played together for a long time. Most of the time we think alike, but there is one thing I really disagree with him about. I think it's wrong the way he lets guys foul him. If a guy did some of those things to me, I'd bust him over the head. But I'm just not as nice a guy as Bobby and everyone knows it."

As the years went on, Bobby grew less tolerant of overzealous young defensemen. He started striking back, using his great strength to ward off his tormentors.

As time passed Bobby also grew more conscious of the future. He had a cattle ranch in Canada that he loved working in the off-season, but he nevertheless wanted to be sure that his family's future was financially secure. Salary squabbles with the Hawk management —including one pre-season holdout—became the norm. And money was certainly the reason he jumped over to the WHA.

That jump, plus a multitude of endorsements and shrewd business investments have given Hull the security he desired. Now he is free to finish out his career pretty much on his own terms. That seems to include playing with the Winnipeg Jets and then perhaps continuing for a while as coach. Should the WHA fail to survive, there'd be an open invitation for Bobby Hull to return to his old haunts. Whether he would or not is an open question.

Some people have said that Hull lacks the complete desire and dedication that some other superstars possess. They say he's in the game for money. There may be a grain of truth in that, but Bobby certainly didn't get where he is today by hating the game.

"I consider myself a fluent performer," Bobby once said. "My moves are fluent, but they didn't get that way by luck. It took work. You can know what you must do out there, but that won't help you a bit unless you can do it automatically. All that takes a lot of time and practice, believe me."

There are plenty of people who can testify to Bobby's desire to excel, teammates who have seen Bobby stay on the ice long after practice, firing puck after puck at the net from all kinds of angles. But hockey is a wearing business that can get to a player after 16 years.

Bobby Hull was *the* hockey player of the 60's, the man who did the most to popularize the game in its period of rapid growth and widespread excitement. He's been overshadowed somewhat in the 70's by the likes of Bobby Orr, Phil Esposito (who broke Bobby's goal-scoring record) and other younger players. But the Golden Jet has the status of a legend.

After all, how many sports superstars will stop at any time to give autographs to a youngster? And how many will take the time to ask an admiring little girl whether her name, Catherine, is spelled with a C or a K? The answer is Bobby Hull, the same man who once excelled in a Stanley Cup series despite a severely strained shoulder and badly broken nose. He was still all over the ice and even got a three-goal "hat trick" in the final game.

"It was the most magnificent performance I'd ever seen," said Black Hawks' owner Jim Norris. "Bobby should have been in the hospital, but instead he was the best man on the ice in the entire series."

Bobby Hull has been the best man on the ice for a long time.

BOBBY ORR

At the end of the 1969–70 hockey season it was time for the National Hockey League to present its annual awards to the top players of the year. First there was the Art Ross Trophy for the league's high scorer. It went to Bobby Orr, Boston Bruins' defenseman.

Defenseman! Who ever heard of a defenseman winning the scoring title? It never happened in the history of the game. Well, it did in 1969–70. Bobby Orr scored 33 goals and collected 87 assists for 120 points, top total in the NHL. Did that mean that defenseman Orr forgot about playing defense?

Next came the James Norris Trophy for the league's best defenseman The winner: Bobby Orr. As a matter of fact, since with his sophomore season of 1967–68, Bobby Orr has won that one six straight times. He's got it locked up.

Now, if a guy takes both the scoring crown and the best defenseman trophy, not much can stand in the way of his being the league's Most Valuable Player, right? Right. Orr also won the Hart Trophy as MVP. What else is available? Well, there's always the Stanley Cup. Sure enough, the Bruins won that, too, and the man leading the way was . . . Bobby Orr. For that he was given the Conn Smythe Trophy.

And Orr wasn't through, yet. After the season he was named Sportsman of the Year by *Sports Illustrated* and then Athlete of the Year by *Sport* Magazine. He also picked up a couple of additional awards, minor stuff, like outstanding athlete in the United States and Canada.

It sounds like the triumph of some grizzled greybeard veteran, who worked for ten years to achieve one fantastic season. But Bobby Orr had just barely turned 22 when the last of the awards rolled in. Whether he could maintain the pace was the question many fans asked. Next season he'll fall apart, they said.

The next season, Bobby Orr scored 37 goals and picked up 102 assists, breaking his own records, in scoring 139 points. All he took that year were the Norris and Hart trophies. He is slipping, said the doubters.

Then came 1971–72, and once again Bobby Orr was the man. He scored 37 goals and picked up 80 assists for 117 points, playing the last half of the sea-

son on a damaged knee. Then in the playoffs he led
his team into the final round with the Rangers, and
dominated the action there, setting a playoff scoring
record of five goals, 19 assists and 24 points. He won
the Norris, Hart, and Conn Smythe trophies when the
season ended. Bobby Orr was at it again.

Robert Gordon (Bobby) Orr is one heck of a
hockey player. In fact, more and more people are already calling the youthful defenseman the greatest
who's ever played the game. He's risen to that stature in
just seven seasons, yet when Bobby Orr begins his
eighth NHL campaign in 1973, he'll be just 25 years
of age. He may very well prove his champions right.
Listen to what these other National Hockey League stars
have to say about him:

"Bobby Orr is the greatest young hockey player to
come into the league since I've been here," said Bobby
Hull, "and that's 15 years. He's a whiz at controlling
the puck. But he's smart, too. If he's trapped, he'll just
give the puck to a teammate, then bust through and
get it back.

"He really streaks on his rushes and there's no way
one man can defense him. Boston isn't the same club
if he's not going well."

Brad Park, considered the league's second-best defenseman, has no illusions. Said the Ranger stalwart:
"Bobby's most effective weapon is his skating ability. He
can skate circles around me and any other defenseman. His speed gives him that extra split second to do
something with the puck. And watch him. He never hip
checks a guy like I do, because he doesn't have to.
When someone moves outside him, he just takes three
steps toward the man and takes the puck away. On
that same play, I'll have to take the guy into a corner
and tie him up. Not Bobby."

Another Ranger, Glen Sather, a former teammate of Orr's, points out: "Orr's the best-conditioned athlete I've ever seen. It would be interesting to see where his strength comes from. There's not an ounce of fat under his skin. He wears the same size clothes I do, a 43 jacket, 31 waist, yet he weighs 20 pounds more than I do."

Then Sather continued, "I've seen him at three different phases of his career. The first year and a half or so he was learning. He got hit pretty often and was frustrated. Then there was a second phase when nobody knew what to do with him. Now they're beginning to understand him and he's really blending in with the rest of the team. He can let the others do more work, but he still controls the game.

"He doesn't beat you because he's Bobby Orr. He beats you because he's the best. If he came out on the ice with a wig on his head and different numbers on his back, he'd still beat you."

Ken Dryden, the goaltender of the Montreal Canadiens, summed it up: "In all the other sports there's a constant argument about who's the best player. Not in hockey. Bobby Orr is so clearly the best. I don't know if there's ever been someone who so completely dominated a team sport.

"In the Bruin game plan all things flow from Orr. He's on the ice more than half the game and always seems to have the puck when he's out there. And he has so many ways of threatening you. He makes you forget your responsibility and concentrate on him. He disturbs, and there's no pattern of defense you can use on him."

Skating, stick handling, anticipation, shooting—Bobby Orr has it all. Still another NHLer added that Orr has a mean streak on top of all the talent. He's surely not a dirty player, but he won't be pushed around. He let that be known even in his rookie year, when he tangled with some of the NHL's best-known ruffians.

Orr certainly doesn't look like a brawler. At 25, he still has the babyface he had as a rookie. Only the crew cut has given way to a thick mop of dirty-blond hair. The face doesn't have the hardened look of a veteran, and the smile is still quick and pleasant. But there's a lot of hockey mileage on Mr. Orr, and his body has felt the toll.

Bobby has already had three knee operations, and some question his durability to last 15 or 20 years. He had his third operation before the 1972 Canada-Russia series, and missed that competition. When the knee seemed slow to respond, some thought Bobby would lose speed. But in the 1972–73 season he seemed sound in the second half; and he took his sixth straight Norris Trophy.

Born in Parry Sound, Ontario, on March 20, 1948, Bobby was on skates quickly, with constant encouragement from his father, Doug Orr. Mr. Orr had been a fine player as a youngster and plenty of scouts had come around when he was about 17. But that was in 1942, and he was soon in the army. When he was discharged, his family was on the way and he gave up the sport.

Still, Doug Orr didn't push young Bobby, he simply guided his son and taught him the fundamentals of the game. Parry sound is located some 160 miles north of Toronto and as the expression goes, baby it's cold out there. Bobby and his father often skated together right on the Sound itself, which was frozen during the long winter.

Sometimes Bobby would be out there with dozens of other youngsters, all trying to get into the action and get the puck. That's when Bobby first started controlling it so well, just trying to keep it away from the other boys who tried to take it. By the time he was six he was in an organized league and moved through the various age brackets from there. Then, when he was just 12, the National Hockey League scouts spotted him for the first time.

Bobby was playing for the Parry Sound team against Gananoque, some 300 miles away near the Quebec border. It was a playoff game, and all the youngsters were really working hard. There was a Montreal scout there along with Wren Blair, today the general manager of the Minnesota North Stars. At the time, Blair was a bird dog for the Boston Bruins.

"The Bruins sent me up there to check on a couple of Gananoque kids," Blair recalls. "I started watching them, but it wasn't long before I noticed a Parry Sound kid, blond-haired kid, in baggy pants. He was controlling the game. No one could get the puck from him and he seemed to be doing whatever he pleased. I forgot all about those Gananoque kids and watched him. I made out a pretty enthusiastic report to the Bruins and they immediately asked me to go down to Parry Sound, and to donate $1,000 to their hockey program."

Two years later the Bruins signed Orr under the old letter-of-intent program. The offer they made was a good one, and Mr. Orr left the decision on signing to his young son. Bobby said yes. He was then the property of the Boston Hockey Club.

It wasn't long before Bobby was playing against boys four and five years older than he was and, as usual, controlling the game. The Bruins were floundering around the basement of the league then and to add some excitement to their hockey program they began publicizing the youngster immediately. Wait till Orr gets here, they said. He'll make the team a winner.

By the time Bobby was 16, he was already something of a national celebrity in Canada. His picture was on the cover of a national magazine and he was being billed as the most remarkable young player to come down the pike since Gordie Howe.

Finally the Bruins stopped waiting. They invited Orr to training camp in 1966 and he quickly showed he was ready. He himself had doubts whether he could play in the NHL at 18, but everyone who saw him outplaying wily veterans in camp knew the kid had it.

Bobby was never a conservative player, but it took a couple of years before he really exploded. He had 11 goals and 20 assists in an injury-plagued second year in which he played in just 46 games. Nevertheless, he was so impressive that he won his first Norris Trophy when it was over.

The third year, 1968–69, he had 21 goals and 43 assists for 64 points, and gave strong indications of what was to come. With the Bruins building a powerhouse team, Bobby let loose the next year, doing things on offense that no defenseman before had ever done.

In the early days of hockey, defensemen never rushed with the puck. They gave it off to a forward and retreated to defend their territory. Eddie Shore was the first to rush occasionally when he had the good chance. And he was a skilled practitioner of it. Doug Harvey, the next great defenseman, didn't rush too often. He didn't have to with the talented Canadien teams he played on. Then came Orr.

In the 1969–70 season Bobby Orr showed that a backliner could effectively become an integral part of the team's offense. He rushed the puck to start offensive plays. But the other team had to watch him. If they gave him an opening, he'd dart through and complete the play himself. He went in deeper and more often than any other defenseman and got away with it.

Some claim that Bobby is sometimes caught short on defense because of his offensive tactics, but his quickness, perception, and skating ability easily compensate most of the time. He has truly revolutionized his position, and has shown that a defenseman can singlehandedly dominate a game.

Former Philadelphia Flyer coach Vic Stasiuk describes the way he did it in a game early in the 1970–71 season.

"We outplayed the Bruins," said Stasiuk, "but we lost 1-0 to *him*. It was simply us versus Bobby Orr. We outhustled and outmuscled them, except when he was on the ice. What it came down to was that he did everything a little bit better than everyone else.

"When our players charged him, he just slipped around them and skated away. When they dropped back to wait for him, he just maneuvered into position for a shot, or passed to someone else in better position. It gets so that you begin looking forward to not having him on the ice. And that isn't very often."

What kind of a man is Bobby Orr? He's achieved an awful lot of fame in a short time, and that can sometimes make a person into something he's not. He may be the most popular athlete in Boston. He's recognized everywhere he goes, both in Beantown and all over Canada. In the circumstances, he cannot live a normal life. Yet Orr has handled it well.

"When I left home," he once told a reporter, "my parents gave me one word of parting advice. They told me not to pretend. There are a lot of people who say very nice things about me, that I'm perfect, a great athlete, all that stuff. But I make as many mistakes as the next guy.

"People always want to know how I can take all the publicity, always hearing all those things said about me. They want to know how it affects me. Now I know some people won't believe what I'm going to say, but I'll say it just the same. Whenever I start feeling a little too good about myself, I think about some other kinds of kids, kids who can't walk downstairs to get a sandwich. How can I complain about anything then? Compared to them, I'm nothing."

In fact Bobby Orr rarely sounds his own trumpet. It's now pretty well known that Bobby keeps many of the good things he does to himself. He'll visit a hospital without publicity, without reporters there to shoot pictures and publicize his kindness. He'll just sit for hours with the kids, talking hockey or anything else they like.

That's Bobby Orr, a young man that Alan Eagleson, his friend and attorney, once called "the most Christian man I have ever known." The average fan may never see this side of Bobby Orr. But he can see Bobby Orr, defenseman. And that in itself is enough of a thrill to last a lifetime.

PHIL ESPOSITO

As great a hockey player as Bobby Orr is, it's difficult to think of him and the Bruins without bringing Phil Esposito into the picture. For Espo and Orr are Boston's gold dust twins, a pair of nonstop scorers who have written and rewritten the hockey record books.

Orr, of course, does it from the backline. Espo operates at center and is the hub of the Bruin attack.

But the two have developed an uncanny knowledge of each other, making them the most devastating point producers in the history of the NHL.

"Orr creates the situation and Esposito puts it away," was how Bobby Hull described the pair. "They know each other's moves by heart and work perfectly together."

Espo started his career in Chicago, centering a line that included the great Hull. You know where that put Esposito . . . second fiddle. Yet he did well, feeding Hull and giving the line muscle around the net. He also scored more than 20 goals in each of his first three seasons.

But that was just a mild warmup compared to what happened next. In what may be one of the most one-sided trades in hockey history, the Black Hawks sent Espo, Ken Hodge and Fred Stanfield to Boston for defenseman Gilles Marotte, center Pit Martin, and goalie Jack Norris. Only Martin has played good hockey for the Hawks, while all three former Chicagoans have become top stars at Boston.

And at the top of the heap was Espo, the 6-1, 210-pound center who has been on the greatest five-year scoring binge in hockey history. His first year with the Bruins, Phil got the feel of the situation with 35 goals and 49 assists. That was good for 84 points and his best year ever. The next season he emerged, scoring 49 goals and adding 77 assists for 126 points, a new NHL record. For his efforts, Espo won both the Art Ross and Hart Trophies that year.

The next season, 1969–70, was Espo's "off year." He had 43 goals and 56 assists for 99 points, relinquishing the scoring title to teammate Orr. But in the

Stanley Cup playoffs that year, the big center got 13 goals and 14 assists for 27 big points as the Bruins won their first Cup in years. Then came the season of 1970–71.

This is the one people have a hard time believing. Espo came out smoking and didn't stop. When it ended, he had obliterated every scoring record there was. He got 76 goals in 78 games, an unheard-of total. Add to that 76 assists for 152 points—and then look again. The next year: 66 goals and 67 assists for 133 points, and in '72–73, 55 goals and 75 assists for 130 points.

Doesn't all that make Phil Esposito one of the greatest centers in hockey history? Seems as if it should, but many hockey buffs say no.

First, they point out that Espo is playing on one of the greatest scoring-machine teams in history. Second, he has Orr to set him up. Third, the league's expansion has given him a chance to score against poorer teams with poorer players. And, last, they say that many of his goals are "garbage" goals, collected from in close at the net. No, they say, he's not a Morenz or a Beliveau. He's not a slick as a Mikita, as smooth as a Ratelle, or as rugged as a Tkachuk.

But then there's the argument on the other side. Every other center in the NHL has had the chance to rival Espo's feats. None has. And it was Phil Esposito whose rugged play and spiritual leadership got the Canadians back into that series with the Russians before the 1973 season.

The point is this. Espo's style of play with the Bruins is not flashy. He doesn't carry the puck as much as some centers, because he has the great Orr to set things up. And he has two rugged wings, Cashman and Hodge, to get the puck out of the corners for him.

Yet Espo's style is deceptive. He absorbs a tremendous amount of punishment. What the big center does is stake out a territory in front of the net, from about 20 feet out and closer. Once there, he waits for the pass or the rebound, and looks to put it in. But it isn't garbage. Many times he must maneuver in very crowded territory, carrying the puck short distances against stiff opposition. And standing in the helter-skelter area in front of the net subjects him to a frequent pounding from enemy defensemen, determined not to let Espo get good position. Much of the pounding goes undetected by the refs. Yet Espo continues to score.

Another fact attests to Phil's all-around ability. The high numbers of assists he collects each year prove that he does more than shoot. He's always trying to set up open teammates, and once again he must make his passes from some pretty tough places, surrounded by the determined opposition.

Phil Esposito is one good hockey player.

A typical Esposito goal was described by Chip Magnus, hockey reporter for the Chicago *Sun-Times*. It was during a game with the Black Hawks several years ago and, ironically enough, came against Phil's all-star goalie brother, Tony Esposito.

"Phil moved into position just off the right corner of the net," Magnus observed. "Then Keith Magnuson (Black Hawks defenseman) belted him a shot and knocked him right into the net post. Just as he recovered, Jerry Korab skated by and pinned Phil's stick with his own, then elbowing Espo and spinning him around.

"Stan Mikita was next. He hit Phil with a hipcheck as he skated past in the heavy traffic. Espo was still holding the territory and Magnuson hit him from behind, digging his shoulder into Espo's lower back. Magnuson pushed him again, but suddenly the puck came inside, Espo got his stick on it and scored."

It isn't easy. The number of times Espo does it during a season would take a toll on the average player, no matter how tough he is. But Esposito knows how to use his body and his skills; he's a wily, intelligent player.

"Espo will be moving around there, nice and slow," said a Bruin teammate. "Then he'll get the puck and suddenly be gone. Sometimes his movements give the impression that he's just a big, slow guy, but he can fool you. Other times he'll just use his strength and beat his man by four or five feet. Only one other guy on our club can do this kind of thing, and that's Orr."

The mild-mannered Espo tires of hearing about his so-called garbage goals. "Let anyone who complains about it try some himself," he'll say. "Remember, there may not be a rule against staying in the area in front of the net, but I'd like to see some guys try to camp there. They'd be surprised at what happens. One night I complained to the ref about what was going on in there and he just laughed at me. So I smiled back. What else could I do?"

Phil Esposito has been smiling for a long time, though his sad eyes sometimes belie his grin. But his mother said he was a happy-go-lucky youngster right from the first. Espo was born on February 20, 1942, in Sault Ste. Marie, Ontario. Both Phil and his brother Tony were on skates early and were signed into the Black Hawk organization while still in their early teens. Espo played Junior hockey with the St. Catharines Teepees in the A division of the Ontario Hockey Association. His final year he scored 32 goals and had 39 assists, making the league's second all-star team. Still, no one trumpeted much about Phil's skills. Bobby Hull who had been with the Teepees several years earlier, was still the ranking hero with the fans. Already Phil was playing in the shadow of legendary stars.

After two seasons with the St. Louis Braves of the Eastern Hockey League, Espo was brought up to the parent club. When he joined the Hawks, the team already had some fine individual players, including Hull, Stan Mikita, Pierre Pilote, and goalie Glenn Hall. Young Phil saw some action during the 1963–64 season and then became a regular the next year. He performed well with Chicago, right up until his trade to Boston.

Phil faces a dilemma unique among hockey players. He must often go up against his own brother, firing the rock-hard puck that can seriously injure a goalkeeper. The brothers are separated by just a year in age and have always been very close.

"Tony and I both know what we have to do. He roots for me except when he's trying to stop me and I always pull for him except when the Bruins play the Hawks. It's got to be that way. I guess our parents have the bigger problem when we're going head to head.

"We do have one rule; we never speak to each other during the playoffs. I've been on the ice when he's been hurt and I avoid going over to him. I wait for another player to come over and let me know he's all right. Then I'll try my hardest to score on him again."

Espo tries harder against everyone. His determination and drive are both integral parts of his game. And he bristles whenever someone says the Bruins run up the score against weak opponents.

"This team doesn't set records because of expansion and weak opponents," he said. "We do it because of our basic offensive philosophy. We hit, get position in front of the net, help each other out, and shoot. Sometimes it burns me when they belittle our records and point to the players of the past. If you want to know what I think, it's that there's never been a hockey club that could tie our skates."

So pride is another factor in Espo's play. He's always been candid, too, about his own abilities. He still calls Bobby Hull the greatest goal-scorer who ever lived, and readily admits that he can't score the way Hull does, on booming slapshots from all over the rink.

"A guy's got to do what he does best," says Espo.

It's not as simple as all that. Perhaps the goaltender is best qualified to evaluate the artistry of Phil Esposito. One of the greatest netminders of all time, Jacques Plante, has nothing but admiration for the Bruins' great center.

"Phil is always trying new things, working on new tricks," said Plante. "Because of this there is no one shot you can look for when he has the puck. He also studies hard. He learns the habits and weaknesses of all his opponents, especially goaltenders, and he plays to their weaknesses. He's a great hockey player."

With what Espo has done in the last five years, there can be little doubt about his greatness. Not any more.

KEN DRYDEN

No matter what period of hockey history you look at, there are arguments about goaltenders. Who's the best? Which one performs best in the clutch? Who's the coolest under fire? When the talk turns to the current crop of goalies, three names usually dominate the conversation—Ed Giacomin of New York, Tony Esposito of Chicago, and Ken Dryden of Montreal.

Giacomin has been around the longest, then comes Esposito, and finally Dryden. The first two are born-and-bred hockey players, always were, and fine netminders at that. Both are shutout goalies, capable of producing a whitewash on any given night. They've been first team all-stars and have excelled for a number of years now.

Then look at Dryden. He's different from the others, in the way he began his NHL career, and in the life-style he chooses. He is a most unlikely goaltender, and in more ways than one.

First of all, Dryden is outsized for a netminder, standing 6-4 and weighing some 210 pounds. Second, he tends goal for the Montreal Canadiens, a team with a history of great goalies of *French* ancestry. Dryden is English. Then there's the fact that he was educated in the States, and college educated, at that, having graduated from Cornell University. That, too, breaks the mold. And it doesn't stop there. Ken Dryden is now attending law school, and he continues to go during the hockey season.

Then there was Dryden's debut. He's the only goaltender, in fact the only player in National Hockey League history, to win the Conn Smythe Trophy before winning the Calder Memorial Trophy.

At the tail end of the 1970–71 season, Ken Dryden was brought up to the Canadiens when the Frenchmen found themselves with a shortage of goalies. Dryden got into just six games, but in those six he yielded just nine goals for a 1.65 goals-against average. Not bad. Then came the playoffs, the pressure-packed Stanley Cup playoffs, where even veteran players have been known to perform below par. No place for a pre-rookie goalie with just six games of NHL experience. That's for sure.

But the Canadiens announced that they would start the young netminder in the opening game of the play-offs. Not only did Dryden start, but he started 19 consecutive playoff games after that and wound up bringing the Canadiens the coveted Cup.

In that series, the young netminder gave up 61 goals for a 3.00 average, but he was so brilliant in the clutch and held up so well under the pressure that he was given the Conn Smythe award as the MVP in the playoffs. Some people said it was a fluke, but Dryden proved them wrong. Playing his first full season the next year, he compiled a 2.24 average in 64 games, compiled eight shutouts, and walked away with the Calder prize as Rookie of the Year. He was also a second-team all-star selection. The career of Ken Dryden had really begun.

How long his career will last has been a prime question among Canadien fans for some time. They aren't used to cerebral players such as Dryden, and they're constantly worrying that Dryden is about to quit hockey. After all, how many National Hockey League goaltenders work for Ralph Nader, the consumer crusader, during the off season? "Ralph Nader is a lawyer with a conscience," Dryden says. "There aren't enough of his kind. He has a tremendous grasp of all kinds of situations and the ability to relate them. He also knows just how and where pressure should and can be exerted. He taught me that one man, anyone, can really make a big difference in a bureaucracy."

One man can make a big difference in a hockey team —if he's Ken Dryden—and he's done it. The way he's done it, playing goal and attending law school full time, defies imagination.

"I think it's a good situation for Ken," says his brother, Dave, who's a goalie with the Buffalo Sabres. "If he played hockey and did nothing else, his intelligence might work against him. There are too many worries and frustrations in the league. But if Ken becomes frustrated by hockey, he's got his school to occupy his time."

How does Ken himself handle the pressure of full-time school and full-time hockey together? "It was most difficult my first year," he says. "I had required courses then, and many of them met in the morning when we had practice. That made it tough. The next year, though, I took electives and scheduled most of them in the afternoon. When we didn't have a game my hockey day ended at noon, so there was no problem. Except at exam time. Then I found I didn't have so much time to prepare for them as I'd have liked.

"I remember one conflict during Christmas of 1971. We had a week long Western trip and I had exams, some while we were on the trip and others right after I got back. Now if I miss an exam I've got to take the consequences. But I can't abandon the Canadiens. I'm a full-time hockey player and must be at all the games, all the practices, all the meetings, everything. What the law school has done, sometimes, is have me take the exam on the road at the same time the other students are taking it at school. If they were taking it at nine back in Montreal, I'd have to take it at six in California."

Just as his brother said, Ken sees some definite advantages in his dual role as hockey star and student.

"I find it good to have other interests beside hockey," he confessed. "And on the other hand it's good to have something other than law school. For instance, I'd have a difficult time spending those long hours with the books if I didn't have hockey practice to look forward to. And at Cornell, I'd almost always have my worst games during Christmas vacation, when there was nothing else to look forward to. Maybe it's nervous energy, but I seem to function better when I have several things to do at the same time."

On the ice, Ken Dryden doesn't give the impression of nervousness. He seems cool as an ice cube. Despite the size, his forte is quickness, and he is known for his sprawling, diving, quick-reacting style of play. He also has one of the quickest gloves in the league, and most hockey people feel the glove save is the best because there's no chance of a rebound.

Ken developed his glovework in a curious way. It happened in his childhood, when he and Dave played neighborhood games in Hamilton, Ontario, where Ken was born on August 8, 1947, making him some six years younger than Dave.

Ken got his first goalie equipment from Dave, who had grown into larger sizes. Both played their first hockey with a tennis ball, instead of a puck, and that's where the great glovework came from. Ken always jokes about the tennis ball, saying it might have saved his hockey career.

"A tennis ball doesn't smart nearly as much as a puck," says Ken. "If I knew then how it felt to get hit with a puck I might have quit. But by the time I found out, I was hooked on goal."

Montreal got the early negotiating right to Ken, but he sent them into a state of shock by turning down a generous offer and tramping off to Cornell for an education. Hockey players just don't normally do that. At Cornell, Dryden worked under Ned Harkness, now the general manager of the Detroit Red Wings. Ken never wasted a moment's time. He had seen too many friends pin their entire futures on making the NHL, and the risks of doing that are high, considering all the youngsters playing hockey in Canada. So he studied every chance he had. Even when the team was on road trips, Ken read and studied while the rest of the guys had a good time.

None of it affected his great goal play. His career mark at Cornell was 76-4-1, and his team won a national championship. Ken graduated from the Ivy League school with a solid B-average in his pre-law major and only signed with the Canadiens when the pact assured him he could go to graduate school full time. He played just 33 games in the minors, posting a 2.68 goals against average for the Montreal Voyageurs in the 1970–71 season. Then the parent club called him up for the final six NHL games and the rest, as they say, is history.

The studious Dryden doesn't limit himself to the study of law. He studies his sport with equal intensity, and his shrewd analysis and keen memory of opposing shooters have made his job a little easier.

"Ken remembers everything about every shooter," claims his brother Dave, who also had a fine 1972–73 season at Buffalo. "His trick is the ability to concentrate on the puck and still see everything else at the same time. Plus Ken doesn't have to guess where a certain player will shoot. He remembers things such as Jean Ratelle of the Rangers liking to shoot high on your stick side or that Red Berenson likes to give a head fake and go to the outside. Ken is aware of this without thinking and can react."

As for Ken, he says much of his style has come from his study of European and Russian hockey.

"They (the Russians and Czechs specifically) approach hockey in a much different way than we do. I really admire their method of coaching and instruction. I think it's better than ours. I can't speak for the other positions, but as a goalie, I never really learned much from a coach. Over there, the best goalies put out an instructional booklet which all young goalies can read and study. This has to help.

"They look at games and at individual players very logically. They'll ask questions like, why does a particular player forecheck as well as he does? Or why is he doing what he's doing? By comparison, we (in the NHL) look at the game sort of haphazardly. The reason may be that there are so many games and practices that teams just can't find the time or the strength to approach the game that way."

That's funny, coming from Dryden, because since becoming a regular in 1971–72, Ken has been the iron-man goalie in the league. He played 64 games that year, more than another other netminder, though he admits the brief periods of rest helped him greatly.

"The schedule's too long," he says, candidly. "The pressure of knowing that you had to play every game for two or three months would be unbearable. I don't see how they did it when they had the one-goalie system."

Yet Ken likes work. He's young, intelligent, and energetic, and one of the best goaltenders in the National Hockey League. And who knows: in a few years, the man representing the NHL players may be Ken Dryden, attorney at law.

FRANK MAHOVLICH

They call him the Big M. He's a National Hockey League veteran of some 16 seasons and he's scored more than 500 goals during his career with three different teams. Yet Frank Mahovlich hasn't had it easy.

Starting as a youngster of such enormous potential that a team once offered a million dollars for him, Mahovlich has had a career of ups and downs, a career that has seen him leave his club twice, completely exhausted, both mentally and physically.

It is only in the past three seasons, since the Big M has come to Montreal, that he has found happiness and contentment, and has been finally recognized as the great hockey player he is.

When Mahovlich came into the NHL to stay in 1957–58, his 6-0, 205-pound size made him one of the biggest players in the league. Hence his nickname. He came to the Toronto Maple Leafs riding on a pile of press clippings from amateur and junior days, and the fans expected a miracle worker.

Indeed, Mahovlich was an impressive figure on the ice. He was a left winger with fine skating ability and a tremendous stride that carried him around defensemen with seemingly little effort. His shot was a cannon, giving him the finishing touch after he boomed in close to the net. There was no way he could miss.

Yet the Big M's career is the perfect example of the usual demands placed on an ice star, and the inner turmoil that these great athletes suffer.

Mahovlich was born in Timmins, Ontario, on January 10, 1938. He started skating as a tot, and quickly began the rapid progression through the age-group leagues. By the time he was in his teens Frank was Toronto Maple Leafs' property and being touted as a future star.

He came up at the tail end of the 1956–57 season for a brief, three-game trial. He didn't show much, scoring just once. It meant nothing, except to the fans of Toronto. They'd heard so much about young Mahovlich that they were already disappointed. Second chances come slow to professional hockey players, especially in the knowledgeable Canadian cities.

The next year Frank was officially a rookie. He was up to stay and was soon taking a regular turn on one of the Leafs' forward lines. He finished the year with 20 goals and 16 assists, a modest point total of 36, but good enough to earn him the Calder Cup as the NHL's Rookie of the Year. Considering that there was a rookie in Chicago that season by the name of Hull, Mahovlich must have really impressed those who handle the voting.

Yet because of the big buildup, there was already unfavorable press coming out of Toronto. Coach Billy Reay told a reporter he had expected more from the Big M. It's hard to say just how that first bit of criticism affected Mahovlich, but his next two seasons were unfortunately very similar to the first. He had 22 goals, then 18, and suddenly all the promise of the early years was beginning to fade.

"They all expected me to be Moses when I came up," Frank said, looking back. "The team was down and they needed a big scorer. With no one else around, I was it. I didn't ask for that kind of pressure, but I got it. I got it all."

The Big M came into his fourth season, 1960–61, laboring under a dark cloud. He wasn't yet 23 years old, but he was being called a has-been. Preseason stories cited his failure to live up to his reputation and began harping on something new. They said he was a terrible defensive hockey player.

"That wasn't fair, either," recalls Frank. "First all the pressure to score, then they say I couldn't play defense, but I wasn't really given a chance."

Still, Mahovlich was young and bounced back. Suddenly, in the 1960–61 season he started to put it together. On November 5, the Leafs were up against the Rangers in Toronto and the Big M finally showed his stuff. He carried the puck with brilliance, stick-handling through and around the hapless Ranger defenders. When he was open, he boomed the big shot in there. Four times the red light went on and Mahovlich raised his hands in the air, the traditional gesture of a score.

In the following weeks, the Big M continue to plaster NHL goalies. By the end of December he had 29 goals in 32 games, and right away comparisons were being made with Rocket Richard and his great, 50-goal season. Frank got his 48th goal with a few games still remaining, but halted there. Still, it was a great season, and catapulted the Big M into the superstar class. Some feel now that it was the worst thing that could have happened to him.

"When Frank scored those 48 goals, it somehow made people feel, almost demand, that he duplicate the feat every year, if not top it," claimed one Toronto reporter. "And the big-money offer didn't help the situation, either."

The "big-money" offer was one million dollars, which the Chicago Black Hawks supposedly were ready to hand to the Leafs in return for Frank. It was said that the Chicago people had visions of Bobby Hull on one line and Mahovlich on the other, blasting opposing goalies for the next 15 years (the two players were the same age). The Leafs said no, but Mahovlich became known as the million-dollar hockey player.

When the million-dollar player fell off to "just" 33 goals the next season, Toronto fans moaned, and new coach Punch Imlach again questioned the drive and ambition of his star. While the Leafs were winning three consecutive Stanley Cups from 1962 to 1964,

Mahovlich's star was fading further into the background. He had 36, 26, and 23 goals during those years—but he was a guy expected to get 50.

Meanwhile the boos were increasing every time Mahovlich stepped on the ice and when he sulked (who wouldn't?) he began getting a reputation as a moody brooder, who rarely spoke or smiled. Once Mahovlich seemed reluctant to fight with a player some five inches shorter than he, and the fans booed him some more.

"Listen," he said, "I'll fight anytime, but what's the use in that kind of situation? If I win, I'm a bully. If I don't, I'm a bum. I'd rather conserve my energy for scoring goals."

None of it helped. In November 1964, Frank was taken to a Toronto hospital, suffering from exhaustion, depression, and tension. It was a mild breakdown. He returned in December to more boos. Some other players around the league began to bristle at the treatment Mahovlich was receiving.

"I think the Toronto fans should begin to appreciate Frank's talents and stop that ridiculous booing and the pressure wouldn't get to him," said Gordie Howe. "The fans are hurting their own team by getting on Frank."

But the situation didn't improve much. Frank had 32 goals in '65–66, then tailed off again the next two years. The trouble came to a head in the '67–68 season. Frank had a great game in Toronto, earning the number two star of the night. When he came out on the ice he was booed. Later that night he left the team and the next day turned up in the hospital again. It was the second time his nerves had caused him to quit.

That prompted the Toronto management to act. They shipped the Big M to Detroit in a multi-player deal. Frank finished the year with the Red Wings. The next season, he came out on a line with Gordie Howe and veteran Alex Delvecchio. And he produced fireworks on the ice. Playing with two other great veterans gave Frank his confidence. He put in 49 goals, his best year ever, and added 29 assists for 78 points. He was once again the superplayer he'd been early in his career.

Although Howe got most of the press coverage in Detroit, some other NHL players began talking about the Big M's multiple talents, which people had always tended to overlook. Said New York Ranger defenseman Harry Howell:

"I think Frank's the toughest man in the league to stop. Players like Henri Richard get by on speed but don't have Mahovlich's strength. A Bobby Hull does it with power but doesn't have Frank's great reach or shift. Jean Beliveau can stickhandle, but he doesn't have the Big M's speed."

In 1969–70, Mahovlich fell victim to the disintegration of the Red Wings, a team with front office troubles. "I've never seen an organization fall apart so suddenly," Mahovlich said. "It was a bad situation and really no fun playing there." Nevertheless he racked up 38 red lights.

Midway through the 1970–71 season, Frank was traded to Montreal for some young players. At first the Big M wasn't sure how he'd get on with the Flying Frenchmen. He'd had two very good years at Detroit.

"I always wondered how it would be in Montreal," Frank said, "but I felt better going there knowing Pete (Frank's younger brother) was on the club. When I arrived, I was surprised to find that Pete wasn't just another player, he was a leader, and that made it easier for me to blend in."

What really made it easy was Frank's play. He got 17 goals the second half of the 1970–71 season, then exploded in the playoffs, leading the club with 14 goals, a record, and tying Phil Esposito's record for total points with 27. In a hockey-crazed city like Montreal, that made the Big M an instant hero, and he finally got the recognition and publicity he deserved.

He didn't let anyone down. Playing relaxed for the first time in his career, the Big M led the Canadiens in the '71–72 season with 43 goals and 53 assists for 96 points. A year later he added 38 goals and 55 assists for 93 points as the Canadiens won their second Cup in three years. The Big M had found a home.

Last season, when he was also chosen an alternate captain of the Canadiens, he said: "That's the first time I was ever chosen for anything since I've been in this game. It showed the other guys respect me and it's a nice feeling to have."

Frank is now the fifth best goal scorer of all time and should soon pass Jean Beliveau and Rocket Richard. Hockey people consider him one of the great ones and he himself is finally happy. A long road, but well worth it. For fans who appreciate seeing a great player, Frank Mahovlich, the Big M, is one of the best.

STAN MIKITA

Like Frank Mahovlich, Stan Mikita was denied full recognition until later in his career. Mikita has spent his career on the same team with the dynamic Bobby Hull, who gets most of the publicity.

That hasn't stopped Mikita from playing outstanding hockey for 15 years. In that time he's scored more than 400 goals and picked up nearly 700 assists, which puts him among the top NHL point-getters in history. He's also won the league scoring crown four times, the MVP twice, and the Lady Byng Trophy for good sportsmanship on two occasions.

In the 1966–67 and 1967–68 seasons, Mikita had 97 and 87 points respectively and became the only player in NHL history to win all three awards two years running. In those years, even the mighty Hull had trouble overshadowing the little center from Czechoslovakia.

Mikita is 5'-9", 165 pounds. He makes up for his lack of size with massive amounts of spirit. One of the Chicago reporters kidded him once about playing second fiddle to Hull.

"When you're number two I guess you try harder, huh, Stan?" said the reporter.

Mikita turned red around the ears. "No man ever considers himself number two in anything," he answered, adding quickly, "especially not me!"

Plenty of people agree that Mikita is no second violin. Though Hull, when he was in Chicago, was the game's most dynamic scorer and one of its top gate-attractions, Mikita had as great, or perhaps greater value to the Hawks. With a player like Mikita centering another line, the team had depth and a one-two punch that was hard to beat.

Furthermore, as a center Mikita was the key man on crucial faceoffs, game after game. And he won them about 85 percent of the time against the best centers in the league.

For years, Mikita centered a line in Chicago with Doug Mohns and Kenny Wharram, two swift wingers. The three men were called the "Scooter Line" and known for their speed and scoring ability. They were also one of the most talkative lines on the ice, constantly shouting and signaling one another. And they helped keep the Hawks in contention for the Stanley Cup year after year. Mohns was finally traded and Wharram forced out of the sport by a heart condition, but in the '60's the Scooter Line was one of the best.

When Mikita first came into the league he was a volatile little guy with a short fuse, fighting and brawling whenever anyone came near him. He bristled at the treatment big Hull got from rival defenseman, claiming he'd bust anyone who did that to him.

And he wasn't kidding. One veteran defenseman, Allan Stanley, talked about Mikita's trigger temper. "All you have to do is give Stan a little job and he reacts immediately," Stanley said. "Other guys, even the rough ones, will wait for a chance to retaliate. Not Stan. He hits back in the same motion. He's an ornery little guy, at that."

During the 1964–65 season, the tolerant Hull won the Lady Byng Trophy as the player best combining skill and sportsmanship. That same year Mikita accumulated 154 minutes in the penalty box, almost leading the league in badman tactics.

Who would have guessed that just two seasons later it would be Mikita winning the Lady Byng Trophy. He had occupied the box just 12 minutes in 70 games.

"I just decided to behave," Mikita says. "It wasn't so hard. Seems like the nice guys are making the money, so I figured I'd like to pick up a few extra bucks."

Mikita was born in Czechoslovakia, in a town called Sokolce, on May 20, 1940. His real name was Stanilas Gvoth, and his family was very poor. His father worked in a textile factory and his mother in the fields. When the Communists took over in 1948, the Gvoths made a courageous decision. They wanted a better future for their son and they decided to try to get him out of the country.

Stan had an uncle and aunt living in Canada. His parents wrote to ask if they would raise the young Stanislas. Joe and Anna Mikita, who were childless, agreed. They visited the Gvoths in Sokolce, and when they left, young Stan went with them.

"Like most kids, I was really excited about going at first," Stan remembers. "But just as the train was ready to pull out, I realized my parents weren't coming and I wrapped my arms around a telephone pole and cried. During the whole trip I was planning to jump off the train and go home." But Stan Mikita was in his new home in St. Catherines, Ontario, by Christmas of 1948.

There, Stan saw youngsters his own age playing hockey right on the frozen street. Stan had already skated on double-runners in his native country, but he had never played hockey. He didn't understand or speak English. When one of the boys gave him a stick, the first thing he did when the action started was belt another boy with it.

But soon Stan knew the rules, and his first words in English were hockey terms. The more he played, the better he got. Before long he was outskating older, more experienced boys who resorted to calling him names, most of them having to do with his foreign origin, and that was also the beginning of Mikita the fighter.

"Sure, I had my share of fights in the streets," Stan said in later years. "As a matter of fact, I've been fighting most of my life."

Finally Stan was good enough to play with the St. Catharines Teepees in the junior league, and in the 1958–59 season he had his first trial with the Hawks,

He became a regular the following year, scoring eight goals and adding 18 assists in 67 games. Although he didn't score much, he managed to find his way to the penalty box for some 119 minutes.

The next season he notched 19 goals, and the year after that 25 goals and 52 assists for 77 points. He had six goals in the playoffs that year as the Hawks won the Stanley Cup, and he made the all-star team for the first time. Mikita was off and winging.

Over the next decade, Stan was steady as a rock. Hull set the scoring records, but many considered Mikita the heart of the team. His forte was stick work, puck-handling, and passing. But he could score, too, and he was a faceoff-artist, and a determined defensive player.

In a game with Montreal during the 1968–69 season Mikita was hit twice from behind and felt something snap in his back. Doctors could not pin down the injury, and Stan continued to play the season despite his pain. He scored 97 points that year, 86 the year after, and 72 in 1970–71.

Then, in '71–72, Stan's pace slowed. He got just 65 points and when he missed a key, open-net shot in the playoffs, the critics said he was on the way down. They said that he'd lost the killer instinct, that he was just playing out the string for his paycheck, that he'd become a temperamental skater who used his bad back as an excuse on the nights he didn't feel like playing.

"I don't really buy that slipping stuff," Stan growled. "I skate just as fast as I ever did, though maybe I'm not as durable as I was once. I know I've learned to live with the back injury, but when we have four games in five nights or something like that, I just can't spend as much time on the ice as I used to."

Still, the stories persisted. Then the Hawks learned

that Hull had jumped to the WHA prior to the 1972–73 season. Suddenly, everyone looked to Mikita to pick the team up. He did. Playing like the Mikita of old, he dominated the action—scoring, setting up teammates, winning faceoffs, killing penalties, and skating rings around younger players. In fact, he was among the league leaders in scoring when he suffered a broken heel and the consequent loss of playing time.

Stan returned for the final weeks of the season after missing 21 games. Despite playing in just 57 contests, he scored 27 goals and added 56 assists for 83 points. Had he played the entire slate he undoubtedly would have gone over the 100-point mark for the first time and might even have challenged Phil Esposito's 130-point league lead.

There was a rumor during the off-season, that Mikita would follow Hull and jump to the new WHA. It is no secret that the Chicago Cougars of the new league would like to pirate Mikita away from the Black Hawks. They're offering big money, and Stan is well past 30; the security must be appealing.

Whether the man the Canadiens fans once called *Le Petit Diable* (the little Devil) jumps or not is in question at this writing. But no matter what he does, or where he finishes his career, Stan Mikita will go down in the books as one of the true superstars of the game.

THE FRENCH CONNECTION

The Buffalo Sabres were born to expansion in 1970–71. Because they were a new team, they had the first pick in the annual amateur draft and chose Gilbert Perreault, a 20-year-old youngster from Victoriaville,

Quebec. Perreault promptly lived up to all his notices by breaking the rookie scoring record with 38 goals and 34 assists for 72 points.

The next year Buffalo once again had a high pick. This time they chose another Frenchman, 20-year-old Richard Martin from Verdun Quebec. Martin was a left winger and he promptly broke Perreault's rookie record with 44 goals and 30 assists for 74 points.

Then the Sabres looked for a right wing to play with Perreault and Martin. During the '71–72 season they had traded with Pittsburgh for a 23-year-old Frenchman named Rene Robert, from Trois-Rivieres, Quebec. Robert scored seven goals for Pittsburgh and six more for Buffalo that year. But when he was put on a line with Perreault and Martin, in 1972–73, Robert suddenly became a terror, scoring 40 goals and adding 43 assists for 83 points.

And so was born "The French Connection," a line of three youngsters who were the best trio in the league during 1972–73. Perreault had 28 goals and 60 assists for 88 points, while Martin's totals were 37 and 36 for 73 points. They captivated the hockey world and led the three-year-old Sabres to a fourth-place finish and a spot in the playoffs.

Rarely has a team come up with three such effective players in a three-year span. Perreault, Martin, and Robert clicked from the first. At this writing, Robert is not yet 25, Perreault not yet 23, and Martin barely 22. It's conceivable that the trio could play together for 10 or 15 years, with a chance to become one of the top lines in hockey history.

Perreault came to the NHL with all the advance clippings. They called him the new Beliveau. Born in the same town as Beliveau, the young Perreault idolized the Montreal star. In fact, were it not for the new draft rule, Gil would have been the property of the Canadiens. But he's happy now in Buffalo, and plans to play there for a long time.

"All I ever wanted to do was be a hockey player," Perreault says. "I try not to copy Beliveau because he was too great for me. It was always my goal to play with him at Montreal but I'm happy things worked out this way. Now there is not so much pressure and I can play my own game."

But he's happy to be compared with Beliveau and works hard to justify the comparison. One of his proudest moments came when people in his home town of Victoriaville changed the name of the local golf tournament from the Jean Beliveau Golf Tournament to the Jean Beliveau-Gilbert Perreault Golf Tournament.

Whether scoring himself or feeding his wings, Perreault is a classic player who keeps fans on the edge of their seats. His game involves brilliant skating, stickhandling, and a variety of "moves" and fakes that baffle even the most brilliant defensemen. In fact, Bobby Orr, the best of the bunch, has said on more than one occasion that Perreault is "easily the most exciting player I've seen come into the league."

Buffalo General Manager, Punch Imlach, has had numerous offers for his young center, and he dismisses them with a quick wave of the hand.

"As far as I'm concerned," Imlach says, "Perreault is the best center in the game—bar none. There's absolutely no way anyone is going to get him out of Buffalo."

Richard Martin, too, is French. Other players were picked before him in the draft his rookie year, but as soon as the Sabres saw him unleash his slapshot, they smiled and were thankful to have him.

Atlanta coach Bernie Geoffrian, a shrewd judge of talent, took one look at Martin firing the puck and said, "He's got the best shot in the NHL, maybe the best I've ever seen."

Punch Imlach, so high on Perreault, values Martin just as much, claiming, "He's the best goal-scorer I've ever coached, and I've had Beliveau and Frank Mahovlich on my teams. Rick is a kid with special talent, those little skills for producing goals that only a few players have. He can do it with an overpowering slapshot, or finesse it in with a quick wrist shot or backhand. He's just got the right touch for doing the right thing."

When Martin scored the 39th goal of his rookie year to top Perreault's record, hockey reporter Jim Coleman wrote: "The puck simply didn't have the opportunity to enjoy the pause that refreshes. As soon as it touched the blade of his stick, Martin propelled it into the lower corner of the net."

Martin hasn't been overwhelmed by the wealth of publicity he received as a rookie.

"There was a lot of talk about me scoring 50 goals," he said. "Sure, that would be super, but I don't set my sights on marks like that. I just want to play well in every game. If I do that, the goals will come."

Martin, like Perreault, showed promise early. He once got 12 goals in a midget-league game showing he knew where the net was, even then.

Besides shooting and scoring, Martin is a deft stick-handler with a knack for getting open. He played with Perreault in the juniors and claims that the two already know each other well.

"It's not hard for me to anticipate what Gil is going to do," he said. "He knows my game just as well, so it works both ways for us. It's great playing on the same line with him."

The third member of the French Connection, Rene Robert, is the most anonymous of the trio. He came to the Sabres without fanfare.

Just 5'-9" and 165 pounds, Robert is the smallest and physically the least imposing of the three. He began his career in 1967–68 with Tulsa of the Central League, then bounced around to Vancouver (when that city was still a minor league), Rochester, Tulsa again, and Phoenix.

He had a brief trial with Toronto then went into the Pittsburgh organization. Playing in 49 games for the Penguins during 1971–72, he scored only seven goals and 11 assists, and didn't really impress the Penguin management. When Buffalo offered a seasoned veteran and tough-guy, Eddie "The Entertainer" Shack for him, the deal was made. Robert got six goals in 12 games with the Sabres at the end of the season, and showed some promise of things to come.

"No one really notices Rene out there," said one Buffalo writer. "He was overshadowed by both Perreault and Martin last year. Yet the guy is very shifty on the ice and has an uncanny knack for putting the puck where it belongs, and that's in the net.

"You may not have noticed this, either. But more often than not when a big goal was needed, it was Robert, not Perreault or Martin, who got it. I'm not saying Rene has more ability than the other two, but he certainly more than holds his own with them."

The French Connection is young, talented, hungry. All three men are winners. They're going to be around for a long time.

THE GAG LINE

Unlike the French Connection, "the GAG Line" is not composed of youngsters just beginning their NHL careers. The GAG's are Jean Ratelle, Rod Gilbert, and Vic Hadfield, of the New York Rangers. They have played together for almost a decade, although the name wasn't coined until 1971–72, when the three players produced one of the most sensational seasons in league history.

Ratelle is the gentleman, the classic player, the soft-spoken family man who likes nothing better than to go home after a game and play with his kids. He's a smooth-skating, skilled passer, who can flick a wrist shot into the net as quickly as you can say "Phil Esposito," the man who has overshadowed Gentleman Jean as the league's best center over the past several years.

Gilbert is the right winger with the big slapshot. Rocket Rod was supposed to be a superstar ten years ago, but he never quite made it. But in the last two seasons he has produced the way people always thought he should. And, perhaps coincidentally, it happened after he decided to get tough with opposing defensemen who have always taken liberties with him. Off the ice he's one of New York's swinging bachelors, seen in all the right places, the "in" bars, living the life of the social set on Manhattan's East Side.

Vic Hadfield is the "policeman," the brawler, the man who goes into the corners and gets the puck for the other two. But Hadfield, also failed to bring his game together until recently. He was always slapshot happy, sometimes firing from 40 feet away. When he learned that his strength would permit him to hang around the net where his quick stick could do real damage, he became a 50-goal scorer and superstar. Off the ice, Hadfield is the team's practical joker, a free spirit who keeps his teammates loose and laughing.

Rod Gilbert and Jean Ratelle were boyhood friends and have played on the same line ever since they can remember. Both played with the Guelph Royals as amateurs and came into the Ranger organization at the same time, 1959. Rod made the big team a couple of years before Ratelle, but when Jean came up they were immediately united on the same line, soon joined by Hadfield, and the GAG's, which stands for goal-a-game, started moving.

There are more similarities between Ratelle and Gilbert. Both have undergone very delicate spinal fusion operations (Gilbert had two) which could have ended their careers. Now, coming into the 1973 season, their statistics are remarkably similar. Ratelle has 267 goals and 377 assists for 644 points. Gilbert has collected 269 goals and 408 assists for 677 points.

Gilbert is the more flamboyant player who scores in bursts and streaks; Ratelle is steady as a rock, perhaps the best everyday player on the Ranger team. "Jean is our straight-arrow," says teammate Brad Park. "I'd say he's the perfect model of what a hockey player should be. He's totally dedicated to the sport and the team, and he plays according to the rules. He wouldn't think of elbowing or belting a guy, or doing anything physical. I'd say he's just a beautiful player."

It took a while for Jean to find himself, or to put it a better way, for all the GAG's to stay healthy long enough to put things together. Ratelle finally emerged with identical seasons in 1967–68 and 1968–69, scoring 32 goals and adding 46 assists each time. After that, he was steady and consistent, right to the big year of 1971.

That year, the GAG's began scoring at a record pace. Ratelle led the way. At the halfway mark of the season he was ahead of Esposito for the scoring lead, but the more dynamic Espo made the all-star team. With 15 games left, Jean was still in the race, having scored 46 goals and 63 assists for 109 points. He would have surely burst past the 50-goal mark and maybe even passed Esposito, but then fate took a hand.

A shot by teammate Dale Rolfe fractured Ratelle's ankle and he missed the last 15 games. That kept the line from breaking the single-season mark for a trio and hurt the team right through the playoffs. Still, Jean did collect the Lady Byng Trophy. During his great scoring season, he spent just four minutes in the penalty box.

After a slow start last year, Jean once again led the team in scoring with 41 goals, 53 assists, and 94 points. A modest guy all the way, Ratelle talks about his line play and the comparisons with Esposito.

"Because we've been together for so long we always know just where each of us will be on any given play," he said. "I don't have to look for Rod or Vic. I can just pass and rely on them being there.

"As for Espo, it's pretty hard to compare yourself to a guy who scores 76 goals. Just being close to him in scoring was a thrill for me. When he retires he'll be remembered as one of the great centers of all time. I consider myself proven as a good center."

To many people, Jean Ratelle is a lot more than that.

Rod Gilbert knows what it's like to play with pain. His bad back has forced him to do that in several different seasons, but in the great tradition of his sport, Gilbert hates to miss a game. He's also had the pain of hearing how he never lived up to his potential. Sometimes that kind of pain is even harder to take.

Rocket Rod, as he's sometimes called, had his first 20-goal season as a 22-year-old in 1963–64. That's when everyone began talking about him as the next great goalscorer in the game. But, somehow, he couldn't get out of the 20's. He had years of 25, 28, 29, 28, then slumped to 16 in 1969–70. There were trade rumors, rumors that he wouldn't take coaching, both squelched by Ranger Coach Emile "The Cat" Francis.

"Rod is a great hockey player and slapshooter," Francis said. "I'm not going to try to change him. Would you ask Bobby Hull not to take the slapshot anymore?"

Yet Gilbert's streakiness continued to irk the fans. When he finally got 30 goals in the 1970–71 season, some of his critics shut up. Then came the GAG year. Rod hit on 43 scores, adding 54 assists for 97 points. His production suffered when Ratelle was hurt, and he himself played with a bad neck the last week. But it was surely a great year.

"I'd have to say I've changed over the years," Gilbert admits. "If I go into one of my slumps and stop scoring, I'll try some new techniques and will listen if anyone has advice for me. There was a time I never listened. But this comes with maturity and things are better now."

Rod followed his big year with another 25-goal season, but he added a career high of 59 assists for 84 points, showing that he's become a complete hockey player. For Gilbert, the best may be yet to come.

There was a time when Vic Hadfield was a pure

brawler. He once led the league in penalty minutes with 151. Now he's older and wiser, and the captain of the Rangers. It takes quite a lot of respect and leadership ability to wear that big C. Vic is of the same generation as his linemates, having been born a day later than Ratelle in that same year (1940). He came to the Rangers in 1961, and although it took him some eight years to reach the 20-goal plateau for the first time, he's always been considered one of the mainstays of the team.

In his career he has 235 goals and 282 assists, not quite up to the others, but he makes up for it in other areas, such as being the policeman and protecting his linemates, neither of whom is as good a "mixer" as Vic.

Hadfield's biggest problem early in his career was getting position for his booming shot, yet when Emile Francis took over as coach of the New Yorkers in 1964, he quickly proclaimed Vic Hadfield as one of just four "untouchables" on the team.

"Vic is the kind of guy you like to have around," said the Cat. "He's tough and we always knew he could score. He kept the guys loose, yet was a winner. It was a tough combination to beat."

Vic changed his style somewhat during the 1971–72 season. Instead of firing the puck as soon as he got it, he worked in closer for the better shot. He also became adept at camping out in front of the net and plunking in rebounds and loose discs. He, too, missed Ratelle late in the season, and himself played with a severely bruised thumb. Yet on the very last day of the season he scored his 50th goal, becoming just the sixth man (then) in hockey history to do it. He finished with 50 goals and 56 assists for 106 points.

Last year Hadfield slowed to 28 goals and 34 assists,

but missed some 15 games with an injury and played hurt in many more. He's got to be regarded as one of the best left-wingers in the league.

A reporter once called one of the Rangers for a newspaper story during a break in the schedule. He reached the player at his home and identified himself.

"Sure, Vic," the player said. "You can't fool me."

The reporter assured the man he was for real.

"I know, Vic," was the reply. "Let's cut the joke, okay?"

Once more the newsman tried, swearing he really was a reporter and telling the player to call him back at his office, which the player did. Finally, the two did the interview. When it was over, the reporter thanked the man and said goodbye.

"OK, Vic," was the answer. "I'll see you at practice tomorrow."

Vic Hadfield will do anything for a laugh. But when he's battling for position in front of that goal, he'll do anything for a score. He usually gets a lot of both.

CENTERS IN THE WINGS: GUY LAFLEUR, MARCEL DIONNE, BOBBY CLARKE

Guy Lafleur, Marcel Dionne, and Bobby Clarke are three of the brightest stars to have come into the NHL in recent years—certain superstars of the future.

Lafleur is a Montreal Canadien, a Frenchman carrying on in a grand tradition. He was born in Thurso, Quebec, on September 20, 1951, and came up to the NHL as soon as the amateur draft was completed in 1971.

Guy came up with all the credentials and the comparisons started. After all, it's not every guy who can score 130 goals, yes, 130 goals, in a single season of junior play. But Lafleur did it, and as one Montreal writer said, "everyone had visions of Beliveau dancing in their heads."

That put the pressure on Lafleur, just as it would on any 20-year-old. But Guy's experience goes back a long way—all the way to the age of four.

"My father started me on skates then," the youngster says. "And I played in every game of every league I could get in, right up until I was 14. That's when I got an offer to join the junior team in Quebec and I jumped at the chance."

Right away Guy was thrown in with 17- and 18-year-olds, but he held his own. In fact, those who remember Guy at Quebec say he saved the junior franchise. The team was losing money steadily until the swift-skating kid with the quick shot came along and turned things around.

Soon, crowds of more than 10,000 people were coming to the Quebec Coliseum to see the juniors play. Lafleur and his teammates became so exciting that the American Hockey League team in Quebec was driven out of business and moved to Richmond, Virginia. Such is the power of a superstar.

The Canadiens knew about Lafleur's magic by then and set their sights on the young center. When they landed him, he was immediately put on a line with super wings Frank Mahovlich and Yvan Cournoyer. "Anyone can do well with those guys," critics said, but Lafleur took a few weeks to get his feet wet. Not anyone can do well, no matter how good the wings. The center still has to make the plays.

It may have been the pressure that caused the slow start. Guy had been compared with Beliveau so often that his junior coach, Maurice Filion, finally said:

"Comparing them isn't fair. It's like saying that Howe was better than Richard, or vice versa. Both are great players, and both in their own way."

Finally, Guy began to fulfill his great promise. He was scoring and making plays, and helping his team to win. When the '71–72 season ended, he had 29 goals and 35 assists for 64 points in 73 games. Not a bad rookie year for anyone, bue especially good when you're playing on such a talent-laden team as the Canadiens, in an arena where the fans are among the most knowledgeable and critical in the world.

Despite missing some nine games with an injury and playing hurt for a while afterwards, Guy still scored 28 goals and added 27 assists for 55 points, fifth best on the Stanley Cup champs. Yet Montreal followers say he hasn't really broken loose. Lafleur is still young and still growing. When he puts it together, really together, one of these days, the rest of the league better watch out!

MARCEL DIONNE

They call Marcel Dionne "Little Beaver." But the stocky 5′ 8″ center of the Detroit Red Wings certainly plays big. Picked right after Lafleur in the 1971 amateur draft, Dionne also began under pressure. He was being touted as the man around whom the Detroit franchise would rebuild.

Blessed with speed, deception, and a quick shot, the native of Drummondville, Quebec, quickly proved he belonged in the big leagues. Playing in all 78 games for the Wings, he scored 28 goals and added 49 assists for 77 points, breaking the rookie point scoring mark held by Gil Perreault. The ironic thing is that neither

Lafleur nor Dionne won the Rookie of the Year prize that season. It went to Ken Dryden, the Canadiens' dynamic goalie.

But that didn't deter Dionne. He played with confidence and assurance in his first full season.

"Everyone is so much quicker in the NHL," he said. "The passes come quicker, the checking is quicker and there's more pressure. That's because everyone is playing for a lot of money."

Detroit Coach Johnny Wilson couldn't stop praising his young center.

"The kid was just 20 years old and before the season was half over he was our leader. And with his style of play, his size helps rather than hurts him. Because he's short he's extremely hard to check, and he's so shifty that he sometimes skates right under defensemen.

"Plus he's a tough kid. I've seen him press 230 pounds and there are plenty of so-called big guys who can't do that."

Dionne, too, is well aware of what he can and can't do with his size.

"I'm no Phil Esposito," he says. "No way I'm going to stand there in front of the net and wait for chippies. I've got to rely on my skating and just kinda get lost in the crowd. I've taken a lot of ribbing about my size, but I'm smart enough not to start swinging whenever someone calls me Froggy or Pipsqueak. I'll just tell them where to go and skate away as fast as I can."

Marcel did a lot of fast skating last season. The Wings acquired Mickey Redmond who promptly got 52 goals and took some of the pressure off Dionne. A relaxed Marcel potted 40 and added 50 assists for a magnificent 90 points in just his sophomore season. There seems to be no stopping the little dynamo who's missed just one game in two years. As the man said, you don't have to be big to be tough.

Bobby Clarke may be last on this list, but he's certainly first in many, many ways. To begin with, he was the first Western Division player to win the Hart Trophy as the league's Most Valuable player. He was also the first expansionist player to go over 100 points in a season. And all that made him first in the hearts of Philadelphia hockey fans everywhere.

As a matter of fact, it might be said that Bobby Clarke won the battle of Philadelphia before the 1972 season even began. That's when the rival WHA Philadelphia Blazers acquired the colorful Derek Sanderson in a bid to take fans from the NHL's Flyers. With the high-living Derek in Philly, some thought the modish-looking Clarke would lose his position as the city's number one hockey idol.

It didn't work out that way. Sanderson was injured early, then became embroiled in a contract dispute, keeping him off the ice. He finally jumped the team and returned to his old haunts in Boston. Meanwhile Clarke, in his fourth season, was playing brilliant hockey and leading the Flyers to a second-place finish in the West.

When he was asked about competing with Sanderson for the fans, the modest Clarke answered truthfully.

"I'm an ordinary guy," he said, "so I guess Derek and I have pretty different kinds of lifestyles. But I was rasied this way and I'm happy about it. I've got a wife, a child, and a mortgage. My house has a small pool and I just drive a Corvette. I don't go in for making commercials and a lot of other appearances because I don't have the self-confidence for that type of stuff.

"Oh, yes. I don't need the extra money, either. I'm

making more now than I ever thought I'd make. I once thought that if I made about $18,000 when I was 23 that would be fine. So this is really great."

Clarke was talking about his $100,000 contract with the Flyers, a pact he proved well worthy of in '72–73. In fact, Clarke has improved in each of his seasons and one wonders where he's going to stop.

A native of Flin Flon, Manitoba, Bobby Clarke was born on August 13, 1949. He played the game early, but was not a superplayer in the age-group leagues as were some of the other young stars. In 1968–69 he was having a good year with the Flin Flon Bombers. But when the draft rolled around he was not a high pick. Had it not been for expansion he might not have made the NHL so soon.

But the Flyers took a chance and elevated him to the big club the very next season. Getting a chance to play regularly, the 5′ 10″, 180-pound center showed a lot of talent and a lot of heart. He scored 15 goals, added 31 assists and finished with 46 points and a lot of fans.

The next year he began to show that he was a complete player, scoring 27 times, assisting 36 times for 63 points. He also killed penalties and worked the Flyer power play. In 1971–72, the slick-skating Clarke really came into his own, scoring 35 goals, picking up 46 assists for 81 points. By now, people were getting on the Clarke bandwagon.

"He's got to be the West's first home-grown star," said one player. "He does it all and can play the game with anyone, and that includes those guys in the East."

Though Clarke sees a great deal of ice time and can certainly take care of himself, some of the bullyboys on the Flyers (the club was the most penalized in the NHL in '72–73) make it their personal business to protect Clarke, and they've let it be known around the league that no one better try any cheap shots on their star attraction.

With the WHA making overtures all over the lot, the Flyers offered their star a new, five-year contract. That made Clarke try even harder. He was thoroughly brilliant all during the 1972–73 season, becoming the leader of the new Flyers, a winning team with designs on the top and perhaps one of the few expansion teams with any kind of chance to do well in the playoffs anytime soon.

When the smoke of the season cleared, Bobby Clarke had 37 goals and a whopping 67 assists for 104 points, placing him second to only Phil Esposito in the entire NHL. And when the voting for the Hart Trophy was completed, the classy Clarke finished on top.

Lafleur, Dionne, Clarke, three exciting young players with big futures in the National Hockey League. And the way these men have been coming out of the amateurs in recent years, can more superstars be far behind?

6   *The International Game*

BY NOW, EVERYONE knows that hockey is a Canadian game. Right? Well, there are others playing on the ice, too. In 1954, the Russians entered international competition for the first time—and promptly won the world championship!

The world championship that the Soviets have so often won since then is the championship of amateur hockey. Obviously, the best players in the world—the Canadians—are mostly pros in the National Hockey League, unable to compete in international play. The national teams of other countries, particularly in Eastern Europe, are subsidized by the state and are—by all but official standards—professionals, also.

For the Russians to be world champions of hockey was a source of great embarrassment for Canadians. Slowly, but surely, wheels began to rumble. Maybe an NHL all-star team, or perhaps the Stanley Cup champs, could and should take on the Russian national team in a true World Series of Hockey.

The dream series was finally arranged for the fall of

1972, just weeks before the opening of the NHL season. It was to be an eight-game matchup, with the first four games played in Canada, the final four in the Soviet Union. Now, thought most Canadians, we'll finally show them who owns hockey.

It had been decided that a Canadian all-star team would play the Russians. This meant that the NHL stars would not be performing with familiar teammates, on familiar lines . . . with players whose ice habits they knew well. The NHL team would have just two and a half weeks to get ready, and since it was coming at the end of the off-season, the players probably would not be in very good shape. The Russians, by contrast, played together some 10 to 11 months of the year and were always in shape. They began getting ready some six weeks before the start of the series.

Since the NHL had negotiated the series, it was ruled that only NHL players could perform. This excluded men who had jumped to the new WHA, and that meant the likes of Bobby Hull, Derek Sanderson, and J. C. Trembley. With Bobby Orr recovering from knee surgery, Team Canada was immediately bereft of its two most dynamic performers, Bobby Hull and Bobby Orr.

Still, Team Canada would be formidable. The team had some big names—Esposito, Mahovlich, Dryden, Hadfield, Savard, Cournoyer, Clarke, Park, Perreault, Martin, Dennis Hull, Berenson, etc. There didn't seem to be any reason for panic.

As for the Russians, most everyone was taking them lightly. Only Ken Dryden, Montreal's law-student goalie, sounded a warning when he noted how seriously the Russians take their hockey. "They study the game much more than we do," he said, "and they help each other to improve."

The Soviets are always in top shape. They play a

fast, hard game, featuring crisp passing, and in-close
wrist shots. No one in Russia or Europe does much
with the slapshot. For that reason, most NHL fans
thought the boomers fired by their heroes would leave
the Russian goalies and defensemen in a state of extreme shell-shock.

At that time, no one was aware of the way in which
the Russians trained. They reported to camp six weeks
before the series, but didn't go out on the ice for a full
week. Their coach, Vsevolod Babrov, said his club
would work on three things first, "physical fitness, psy-
chological fitness, and courage." Combine this with
technical skills, and the Russians felt they'd be ready

The team played basketball, tossed around a medi-
cine ball, then did weight lifting and gymnastics. Then
they played hockey on a hardwood floor. In this
drill, the players passed around weighted pucks and
used lead sticks. Their goalies practiced by having a
shot-cannon fire pucks at speeds up to 130 miles an
hour. They may not have used the slapshot, but they
were sure ready to defend against it.

Game one was held in early September at the famous Forum in Montreal. A capacity crowd jammed
the ancient rink to see their heroes put the Russians to
shame. They were on their feet and screaming as Team
Canada took the opening faceoff. Seconds later Frank
Mahovlich fired a shot at Soviet goalie Vladislav Tretiak, a 20-year-old kid who was supposed to be awful.
He stopped the shot, but Phil Esposito was in his
favorite spot and put home the rebound. After just 30
seconds, Canada led, 1-0, and everyone figured the rout
was on.

Five minutes later the Canadians scored again, and
the fans relaxed. It was going to be as easy as they

all hoped and prayed it would. But Phil Esposito noted a strange thing after the second Team Canada score.

"Here these guys (the Russians) were down by two goals, playing on strange ice in a foreign country and they looked as fresh as when the game started. It was almost 90 degrees in the Forum and I sensed that they were in good condition and we weren't."

Esposito's fears were justified. In the next few minutes the pattern of the game was established. The Russians were sprinting up ice every time they got the puck, and slowly leaving the Canadians in their wake. Their short, crisp passing in front of the net baffled the defense and goalie Dryden. The Russians started to score and they didn't stop. When it was over, the Soviet National Team had beaten the National Hockey League all-stars, 7-3. All of Canada was stunned to silence.

The Russians completely outplayed the Canadians. Most observers agreed that Russia's Valery Kharlamov was the best player on the ice and that goalie Tretiak had been superb. Suddenly, the series was desperate.

Game two was played in Toronto. Team Canada decided to get tough, trying to slow the Soviets' fast break. Coach Harry Sinden also united teammates wherever possible. Esposito, for instance, was put on a line with his Bruin teammate, Wayne Cashman, and things worked out pretty well. With Tony Esposito in the nets, Team Canada won, 4-1, and Canada drew breath once again.

Then came disaster. The Canadians were leading, 4-2, in game three at Winnipeg, but tired again and had to settle for a tie. When the club reached Vancouver for game four, Canadian fans had had it. They booed their heroes on the streets, claimed that their national pride was stained, and actually began cheering Russian goals to show their contempt.

The Vancouver game was a shambles. The well-organized Russians grabbed a quick, two-goal lead and went on to win, 5-3. The Soviets had taken the Canadian phase of the series, 2-1-1, and now were going home to put it away.

That's how it looked at the start. Game one in Moscow followed a familiar pattern. Canada had the lead at 3-0 and then 4-1, but once again fell apart down the homestretch and the Russians took it, 5-4, much to the delight of their screaming fans. The Canadian players were becoming discouraged.

"Give the Russians a football and I bet they'd win the Super Bowl in two years," joked Mahovlich. Yet Esposito saw some cause for optimism. He noted that the Russian players were rougher, even dirtier at home, and their kicking tactics, among other things, served to unite the Canadians. Espo also felt that the game finally put Team Canada in good playing shape.

"I honestly felt there was no way we'd lose another," he said.

Still, there was infighting on the Canadian team. The squad numbered some 35 players and they all couldn't suit up for the games. There was grumbling from the start about who should play and who shouldn't. It came to a head in Moscow when several players jumped the team and headed home. They claimed they weren't doing any good to Team Canada and they might as well join their regular teams.

The players who remained pulled together. Toronto's Paul Henderson won the sixth game with a 35-foot slap shot. Esposito scored two early goals in the seventh, but it was Henderson again who broke a 3-3 deadlock by beating Tretiak on a strong individual effort late in the game. Now the series was tied, 3-3-1, and the eighth game would be the clincher.

Both teams went all out from the start. The Russians weren't pushovers. Playing their usual rushing and passing game, the Soviets connected on three power-play goals to take a 5-3 lead into the final period.

Then Esposito got one back at 2:27 of the final session. With about seven minutes left, Brad Park hit Yvan Cournoyer with a perfect pass and the little Montreal winger put in the tying goal. Now it was a matter of getting the last one. The Russians had already claimed that if the game ended in a tie, they'd win the series on the basis of total goals. The Canadians wanted no part of such a debatable situation.

With one minute left the tie looked inevitable. Then Team Canada had the puck. It went into the corner. Both Esposito and Cournoyer were after it. Somehow, Cournoyer got it and centered it. Henderson was alone in front of the net.

He shot. Tretiak made the save. But Henderson got a second chance on the rebound, and he put the disk through the legs of the sprawling goaltender. With just 34 seconds remaining, Team Canada had pulled out the series, with Paul Henderson the unlikely hero.

Why was the series so closely fought? You might say that the Canadians were out of shape and unaccustomed to playing with one another. Maybe. But no one will deny that the Russians can play hockey. So can the Czechs, the East Germans, and several other European countries. The Western European countries are improving, too. Hockey is well on its way to being a truly international sport.

It was Ken Dryden who put it best as Team Canada left Moscow.

"The Russians have gone from nothing to a world hockey power in just 20 years. In that same period of time, Canada has practically stood still. Now it's time for us to make some real progress on our own."

It's hard to say just what form that progress will take. Perhaps there is too much emphasis on wide-open, high-scoring, slapshot-trading games in the NHL now. The game may have lost some of its purity, the passing, stickhandling, faking. The superstars can still do it, but as the Russians showed, everyone should be able to.

There's been some talk about a European Division of the National Hockey League some day. It could happen. Travel would be a problem, but it could be solved. Many details would have to be worked out, such as standardization of rules and impartial officiating. But it could happen.

It is also possible that the future will bring an influx of European and Soviet players into the NHL and even the WHA, since those players have proven themselves of equal or almost equal quality. Then again, there is the problem of the different forms of government and the importance each puts on its athletes.

For hockey is truly a money game now, and a big-money game at that. It has exploded almost overnight, and the cash registers are ringing loudly all over North America. The fans love it. Yet the game is more than a money machine. It is rich in tradition and in a history of legendary players who seem greater with each passing year. Today's stars rival them in many ways.

The rich traditions should continue in future years. That is, unless the hockey explosion becomes an overinflated blowout. But right now the world's fastest game is everywhere. It's come a long way from the frozen icebanks of Canada, and there have been many great moments, every step of the way.